EPIDEMIOLOGICAL HISTORY OF THE WORLD

WORST DISEASE OUTBREAKS IN THE HISTORY

SUBHANSHU YADAV

ISBN 979-888569672-2

Contents

About The Author

Subhanshu Yadav is a class 9 student studying in Delhi Public School Greater Noida. He likes playing table tennis, reading books, and learning about peculiar things. When he was reading about virology and epidemiology, he got the idea to write this book. He learned from edX and Coursera to gather information about this book. He also took help from research literature available in the local library. Biology is not the only subject he likes to engage in. He is also interested in Robotics & IoT. Subhanshu has attended several programs and internships to learn more about his field of interest. Writing down his thoughts is one of his hobbies. He also studies from lectures available on MIT OpenCourseWare.

CHAPTER ONE

THE BLACK DEATH

The Black Death (also known as the Pestilence, the Great Mortality, or the Plague) was a bubonic plague pandemic occurring in Afro-Eurasia from 1346 to 1353. It is the most fatal pandemic recorded in human history, causing the death of 75–200 million people in Eurasia and North Africa, peaking in Europe from 1347 to 1351. Bubonic plague is caused by the bacterium *Yersinia pestis* spread by fleas, but it can also take a secondary form where it is spread person-to-person contact via aerosols causing septicaemic or pneumonic plagues.

The Black Death was the beginning of the second plague pandemic. The plague created religious, social, and economic upheavals, with profound effects on the course of European history.

The origin of the Black Death is disputed. The pandemic originated either in Central Asia or East Asia but its first definitive appearance was in Crimea in 1347. From Crimea, it was most likely carried by fleas living on the black rats that traveled on Genoese ships, spreading through the Mediterranean Basin and reaching Africa, Western Asia, and the rest of Europe via Constantinople, Sicily, and the Italian Peninsula. There is evidence that once it came ashore, the Black Death mainly spread person-to-person as pneumonic plague, thus explaining the quick inland spread of the epidemic, which was faster than would be expected if the primary vector was rat fleas causing bubonic plague.

The Black Death was the second great natural disaster to strike Europe during the Late Middle Ages (the first one being the Great Famine of 1315–1317) and is estimated to have killed 30 percent to 60 percent of the European population. The plague might have reduced the world population from c. 475 million to 350–375 million in the 14th century. There were further outbreaks throughout the Late Middle Ages and, with other contributing factors (the Crisis of the Late Middle Ages), the European population did not regain its level from 1300 until 1500. Outbreaks of the plague recurred around the world until the early 19th century.

Bubonic plague is one of three types of plague caused by the plague bacterium (*Yersinia pestis*). One to seven days after exposure to the bacteria, flu-like symptoms develop. These symptoms include fever, headaches, and vomiting, as well as swollen and painful lymph nodes occurring in the area closest to where the bacteria entered the skin. Occasionally, swollen lymph nodes, known as "buboes," may break open.

The three types of plague are the result of the route of infection: bubonic plague, septicemic plague, and pneumonic plague. Bubonic plague is mainly spread by infected fleas from small animals. It may also result from exposure to the body fluids from a dead plague-infected animal. Mammals such as rabbits, hares, and some cat species are susceptible to bubonic plague and typically die upon contraction. In the bubonic form of plague, the bacteria enter through the skin through a flea bite and travel via the lymphatic vessels to a lymph node, causing it to swell. Diagnosis is made by finding the bacteria in the blood, sputum, or fluid from lymph nodes.

Prevention is through public health measures such as not handling dead animals in areas where plague is common. While vaccines against the plague have been developed, the World Health Organization recommends that only high-risk groups, such as certain laboratory personnel and health care workers, get inoculated. Several antibiotics are effective for treatment, including streptomycin, gentamicin, and doxycycline.

Without treatment, plague results in the death of 30% to 90% of those infected. Death, if it occurs, is typically within 10 days. With treatment, the risk of death is around 10%. Globally between 2010 and 2015, there were 3,248 documented cases, which resulted in 584 deaths. The countries with the greatest number of cases are the Democratic Republic of the Congo, Madagascar, and Peru.

The plague was the cause of the Black Death that swept through Asia, Europe, and Africa in the 14th century and killed an estimated 50 million people, including about 25% to 60% of the European population. Because the plague killed so many of the working population, wages rose due to the demand for labor. Some historians see this as a turning point in European economic development. The disease was also responsible for the Plague of Justinian, originating in the Eastern Roman Empire in the 6th century CE, as well as the third epidemic, affecting China, Mongolia, and India, originating in the Yunnan Province in 1855. The term bubonic is derived from the Greek word βουβών, meaning "groin".

NAMES

European writers contemporary with the plague described the disease in Latin as pestis or pestilentia, 'pestilence'; epidemia, 'epidemic'; mortalitas, 'mortality'. In English before the 18th century, the event was called the "pestilence" or "great pestilence", "the plague" or the "great death". After the pandemic "the furste moreyn" (first murrain) or "first pestilence" was applied, to distinguish the mid-14th century phenomenon from other infectious diseases and epidemics of plague. The 1347 pandemic plague was not referred to specifically as "black" in the 14th or 15th[contradictory] centuries in any European language, though the expression "black death" had occasionally been applied to fatal disease beforehand.

"Black Death" was not used to describe the plague pandemic in English until the 1750s; the term is first attested in 1755, where it translated Danish: den sorte død, lit. 'the black death. This expression as a proper name for the pandemic had been popularized by Swedish and Danish chroniclers in the 15th and early 16th centuries, and in the 16th and 17th centuries were transferred to other languages as a calque: Icelandic: svarti dauði, German: der Schwarze Tod, and French: la mort noire. Previously, most European languages had named the pandemic a variant or calque of the Latin: Magna mortalitas, lit. 'Great Death'.

The phrase 'black death' – describing Death as black – is very old. Homer used it in the Odyssey to describe the monstrous Scylla, with her mouths "full of black Death" (Ancient Greek: πλεῖοι μέλανος Θανάτοιο, romanized: pleîoi mélanos Thanátoio). Seneca the Younger may have been the first to describe an epidemic as 'black death', (Latin: mors atra) but only about the acute lethality and dark prognosis of the disease. The 12th–13th-century French physician Gilles de Corbeil had already used atra mors to refer to a "pestilential fever" (febris pestilentialis) in his work On the Signs and Symptoms of Diseases (De signis et symptomatibus aegritudium). The phrase mors nigra, 'black death', was used in 1350 by Simon de Covino (or Couvin), a Belgian astronomer, in his poem "On the Judgement of the Sun at a Feast of Saturn" (De judicio Solis in convivio Saturni), which attributes the plague to astrological conjunction of Jupiter and Saturn. His use of the phrase is not connected unambiguously with the plague pandemic of 1347 and appears to refer to the fatal outcome of the disease.

The historian Cardinal Francis Aidan Gasquet wrote about the Great Pestilence in 1893 and suggested that it had been "some form of the ordinary Eastern or bubonic plague". In 1908, Gasquet claimed that the use of the name atra mors for the 14th-century epidemic first appeared in a 1631 book on Danish history by J. I. Pontanus: "Commonly and from its effects, they called it the black death" (Vulgo & ab effectu atram mortem vocitabant).

CAUSES

EARLY THEORY

The most authoritative contemporary account is found in a report from the medical faculty in Paris to Philip VI of France. It blamed the heavens, in the form of a conjunction of three planets in 1345 that caused a "great pestilence in the air" (miasma theory). Muslim religious scholars taught that the pandemic was a "martyrdom and mercy" from God, assuring the believer's place in paradise. For non-believers, it was a punishment. Some Muslim doctors cautioned against trying to prevent or treat a disease sent by God. Others adopted preventive measures and treatments for plague used by Europeans. These Muslim doctors also depended on the writings of the ancient Greeks.

PREDOMINANT MODERN THEORY

Due to climate change in Asia, rodents began to flee the dried-out grasslands to more populated areas, spreading the disease. The plague disease, caused by the bacterium Yersinia pestis, is enzootic (commonly present) in populations of fleas carried by ground rodents, including marmots, in various areas, including Central Asia, Kurdistan, Western Asia, North India, Uganda, and the western United States.

Y. pestis was discovered by Alexandre Yersin, a pupil of Louis Pasteur, during an epidemic of bubonic plague in Hong Kong in 1894; Yersin also proved this bacillus was present in rodents and suggested the rat was the main vehicle of transmission. The mechanism by which Y. pestis is usually transmitted was established in 1898 by Paul-Louis Simond and was found to involve the bites of fleas whose midguts had become obstructed by replicating Y. pestis several days after feeding on an infected host. This blockage starves the fleas and drives them to aggressive feeding behavior and attempts to clear the blockage by regurgitation, resulting in thousands of plague bacteria being flushed into the feeding site, infecting the host. The bubonic plague mechanism was also dependent on two populations of rodents: one resistant to the disease, which acts as hosts, keeping the disease endemic, and a second that lacked resistance. When the second population dies, the fleas move on to other hosts, including people, thus creating a human epidemic.

The rate of mortality from the Black Death varied from place to place: whereas some districts, such as the duchy of Milan, Flanders, and Béarn, seem to have escaped comparatively lightly, others, such as Tuscany, Aragon, Catalonia, and Languedoc, were very hard-hit. Towns, where the danger of contagion was greater, were more affected than the countryside, and within the towns, the monastic communities provided the highest incidence of victims. Even the great and powerful, who were more capable of flight, were struck down: among royalty, Eleanor, queen of Peter IV of Aragon, and King Alfonso XI of Castile succumbed, and Joan, daughter of the English king Edward III, died at Bordeaux on the way to her wedding with Alfonso's son. Canterbury lost two successive archbishops, John de Stratford and Thomas Bradwardine; Petrarch lost not only Laura, who inspired so many of his poems, but also his patron, Giovanni Cardinal Colonna. The papal court at Avignon was reduced by one-fourth. Whole communities and families were sometimes annihilated.

DNA EVIDENCE

Definitive confirmation of the role of Y. pestis arrived in 2010 with a publication in PLOS Pathogens by Haensch et al. They assessed the presence of DNA/RNA with polymerase chain reaction (PCR) techniques for Y. pestis from the tooth sockets in human skeletons from mass graves in northern, central and southern Europe that were associated archaeologically with the Black Death and subsequent resurgences. The authors concluded that this new research, together with prior analyses from the south of France and Germany, "ends the debate about the cause of the Black Death, and unambiguously demonstrates that Y. pestis was the causative agent of the epidemic plague that devastated Europe during the Middle Ages". In 2011, these results were further confirmed with genetic evidence derived from Black Death victims in the East Smithfield burial site in England. Schuenemann et al. concluded in 2011 "that the Black Death in medieval Europe was caused by a variant of Y. pestis that may no longer exist".

Later in 2011, Bos et al. reported in Nature the first draft genome of Y. pestis from plague victims from the same East Smithfield cemetery and indicated that the strain that caused the Black Death is ancestral to most modern strains of Y. pestis.

Since this time, further genomic papers have further confirmed the phylogenetic placement of the Y. pestis strain responsible for the Black Death as both the ancestor of later plague epidemics including the third plague pandemic and as the descendant of the strain responsible for the Plague of Justinian. In addition, plague genomes from significantly earlier in prehistory have been recovered.

DNA taken from 25 skeletons from 14th century London have shown plague is a strain of Y. pestis almost identical to that which hit Madagascar in 2013.

ALTERNATIVE EXPLANATIONS

It is recognized that an epidemiological account of plague is as important as an identification of symptoms, but researchers are hampered by the lack of reliable statistics from this period. Most work has been done on the spread of the disease in England, and even estimates of the overall population at the start vary by over 100% as no census was undertaken in England between the time of publication of the Domesday Book of 1086 and the poll tax of the year 1377. Estimates of plague victims are usually extrapolated from figures for the clergy.

Mathematical modeling is used to match the spreading patterns and the means of transmission. Research in 2018 challenged the popular hypothesis that "infected rats died, their flea parasites could have jumped from the recently dead rat hosts to humans". It suggested an alternative model in which "the disease was spread from human fleas and body lice to other people". The second model claims to better fit the trends of death toll because the rat-flea-human hypothesis would have produced a delayed but very high spike in deaths, which contradicts historical death data.

Lars Walløe complains that all of these authors "take it for granted that Simond's infection model, black rat flea human, which was developed to explain the spread of plague in India, is the only way an epidemic of Yersinia pestis infection could spread", whilst pointing to several other possibilities. Similarly, Monica Green has argued that greater attention is needed to the range of (especially non-commensal) animals that might be involved in the transmission of plague.

Archaeologist Barney Sloane has argued that there is insufficient evidence of the extinction of numerous rats in the archaeological record of the medieval waterfront in London and that the disease spread too quickly to support the thesis that *Y. pestis* was spread from fleas on rats; he argues that transmission must have been person to person. This theory is supported by research in 2018 which suggested transmission was more likely by body lice and fleas during the second plague pandemic.

SUMMARY

Although academic debate continues, no single alternative solution has achieved widespread acceptance. Many scholars arguing for Y. pestis as the major agent of the pandemic suggest that its extent and symptoms can be explained by a combination of bubonic plague with other diseases, including typhus, smallpox, and respiratory infections. In addition to the bubonic infection, others point to additional septicaemic (a type of "blood poisoning") and pneumonic (an airborne plague that attacks the lungs before the rest of the body) forms of plague, which lengthen the duration of outbreaks throughout the seasons and help account for its high mortality rate and additional recorded symptoms. In 2014, Public Health England announced the results of an examination of 25 bodies exhumed in the Clerkenwell area of London, as well as of wills registered in London during the period, which supported the pneumonic hypothesis. Currently, while osteoarcheologists have conclusively verified the presence of Y. pestis bacteria in burial sites across northern Europe through examination of bones and dental pulp, no other epidemic pathogen has been discovered to bolster the alternative explanations. In the words of one researcher: "Finally, plague is a plague."

CHRONOLOGY

JUSTINIAN PLAGUE OF 541-544

The first great pandemic of bubonic plague where people were recorded as suffering from the characteristic buboes and septicaemia was the Justinian Plague of 541 CE, named after Justinian I, the Roman emperor of the Byzantine Empire at the time. The epidemic originated in Ethiopia in Africa and spread to Pelusium in Egypt in 540. It then spread west to Alexandria and east to Gaza, Jerusalem and Antioch, then was carried on ships on the sea trading routes to both sides of the Mediterranean, arriving in Constantinople (now Istanbul) in the autumn of 541.

The Byzantine court historian, Procopius of Caesarea, in his work History of the Wars, described people with fever, delirium, and buboes He wrote that the epidemic was one 'by which the whole human race came near to be annihilated'. Procopius wrote of the symptoms of the disease :

" ... with the majority, it came about that they were seized by the disease without becoming aware of what was coming either through a waking vision or a dream. ... They had a sudden fever, some when just roused from sleep, others while walking about, and others while otherwise engaged, without any regard to what they were doing. And the body showed no change from its previous color, nor was it hot as might be expected when attacked by a fever, nor indeed did any inflammation set in, but the fever was of such a languid sort from its commencement and up till evening that neither to the sick themselves nor to a physician who touched them would it afford any suspicion of danger. It was natural, therefore, that not one of those who had contracted the disease expected to die from it. But on the same day in some cases, in others on the following day, and the rest not many days later, a bubonic swelling developed; and this took place not only in the particular part of the body which is called bourbon, that is, "below the abdomen," but also inside the armpit, and in some cases also beside the ears, and at different points on the thighs."

The focus of the Justinian pandemic was Constantinople, reaching a peak in the spring of 542 with 5,000 deaths per day in the city, although some estimates vary to 10,000 per day, and it went on to kill over a third of the city's population. Victims were too numerous to be buried and were stacked high in the city's churches and city wall towers, their Christian doctrine preventing their disposal by cremation. Over the next three years, the plague raged through Italy, southern France, the Rhine valley, and Iberia. The disease spread as far north as Denmark and west to Ireland, then further to Africa, the Middle East, and Asia Minor. Between the years 542 and 546 epidemics in Asia, Africa, and Europe killed nearly 100 million people.

The pandemic had a drastic effect and permanently changed the social fabric of the Western world. It contributed to the demise of Justinian's reign. Food production was severely disrupted and an eight-year famine followed. The agrarian system of the empire was restructured to eventually become the three-field feudal system. The social and economic disruption caused by the pandemic marked the end of Roman rule and led to the birth of culturally distinctive societal groups that later formed the nations of medieval Europe.

Further major outbreaks occurred throughout Europe and the Middle East over the next 200 years – in Constantinople in the years 573, 600, 698, and 747, in Iraq, Egypt, and Syria in the years 669, 683, 698, 713, 732, and 750 and Mesopotamia in 686 and 704. In 664 plague laid waste to Ireland, and in England, it came to be known as the Plague of Cadwaladyr's Time, after a Welsh king who contracted plague but survived it in 682. The plague continued in intermittent cycles in Europe into the mid-8th century and did not re-emerge as a major epidemic until the 14th century.

THE BLACK DEATH OF EUROPE IN 1347-1352

The Black Death of 1347 was the first major European outbreak of the second great plague pandemic that occurred over the 14th to 18th centuries. In 1346 it was known in the European seaports that a plague epidemic was present in the East. In 1347 the plague was brought to the Crimea from Asia Minor by the Tartar armies of Khan Janibeg, who had laid siege to the town of Kaffa (now Feodosiya in Ukraine), a Genoese trading town on the shores of the Black Sea. The siege of the Tartars was unsuccessful and before they left, from a description by Gabriel de Mussis from Piacenza, in revenge they catapulted over the walls of Kaffa corpses of people who had died from the Black Death. In a panic, the Genoese traders fled in galleys with 'sickness clinging to their bones' to Constantinople and across the Mediterranean to Messina, Sicily, where the great pandemic of Europe started. By 1348 it had reached Marseille, Paris, and Germany, then Spain, England, and Norway in 1349, and eastern Europe in 1350. The Tartars left Kaffa and carried the plague away with them spreading it further to Russia and India.

A description of symptoms of the plague was given by Giovanni Boccaccio in 1348 in his book Decameron, a set of tales of a group of Florentines who secluded themselves in the country to escape the plague :

".. in men and women alike it first betrayed itself by the emergence of certain tumors in the groin or armpits. Some of which grew as large as a common apple, others as an egg, some more, some less, which the common folk called gavocciolo. From the two said parts of the body this deadly gavocciolo soon began to propagate and spread itself in all directions indifferently; after which the form of the malady began to change, black spots or livid making their appearance in many cases on the arm or the thigh or elsewhere,.."

The term "Black Death" was not used until much later in history and 1347 was simply known as "the pestilence" or "pestilentia", and there are various explanations of the origin of the term. Butler states the term refers to the haemorrhagic purpura and ischaemic gangrene of the limbs that sometimes ensued from septicaemia. Ziegler17 states it derives from the translation of the Latin pestis atra or atra mors, 'atra' meaning 'terrible' or 'dreadful', the connotation of which was 'black', and 'mors' meaning 'death', and so 'atra mors' was translated as meaning 'black death'.

THE SOCIAL IMPACTS OF THE BLACK DEATH IN EUROPE DURING THE 14TH CENTURY

The overall mortality rate varied from city to city, but in places such as Florence as observed by Boccaccio up to half the population died, the Italians calling the epidemic the mortalega grande, 'the great mortality. People died with such rapidity that proper burial or cremation could not occur, corpses were thrown into large pits and putrefying bodies lay in their homes and the streets. People were as much afraid they would suffer a spiritual death as they were a physical death since there was no clergy to perform burial rites:

"Shrift there was none; churches and chapels were open, but neither priest nor penitents entered – all went to the charnelhouse. The sexton and the physician were cast into the same deep and wide grave; the testator and his heirs and executors were hurled from the same cart into the same hole together."

Transmission of the disease was thought to be by miasmas, disease-carrying vapors emanating from corpses and putrescent matter or the breath of an infected or sick person. Others thought the Black Death was a punishment from God for their sins and immoral behavior or was due to astrological and natural phenomena such as earthquakes, comets, and conjunctions of the planets. People turned to patron saints such as St Roch and St Sebastian or the Virgin Mary or joined processions of flagellants whipping themselves with nail embedded scourges and incanting hymns and prayers as they passed from town to town.

"When the flagellants – they were also called cross brethren and cross-bearers – entered a town, a borough, or a village in a procession their entry was accompanied by the pealing of bells, singing, and a huge crowd of people. As they always marched two abreast, the procession of the numerous penitents reached farther than the eye could see."

The only remedies were the inhalation of aromatic vapors from flowers and herbs such as rose, theriaca, aloe, thyme, and camphor. Soon there was a shortage of doctors which led to a proliferation of quacks selling useless cures and amulets and other adornments that claimed to offer magical protection.

In this second pandemic, the plague again caused great social and economic upheaval. Often whole families were wiped out and villages abandoned. Crops could not be harvested, traveling and trade became curtailed, and food and manufactured goods became short. As there was a shortage of labor, surviving villager laborers, the 'villains', extorted exorbitant wages from the remaining aristocratic landowners. The villeins prospered and acquired land and property. The plague broke down the normal divisions between the upper and lower classes and led to the emergence of a new middle class. The plague lead to a preoccupation with death as evident from macabre artworks such as the 'Triumph of Death' by Pieter Breughel the Elder in 1562, which depicted in a panoramic landscape army of skeletons killing people of all social orders from peasants to kings and cardinals in a variety of macabre and cruel ways.

In the period 1347 to 1350, the Black Death killed a quarter of the population in Europe, over 25 million people, and another 25 million in Asia and Africa. Mortality was even higher in cities such as Florence, Venice, and Paris where more than half succumbed to the plague. A second major epidemic occurred in 1361, the pestis secunda, in which 10 to 20% of Europe's population died.13 Other virulent infectious disease epidemics with high mortalities occurred during this time such as smallpox, infantile diarrhea, and dysentery. By 1430, Europe's population was lower than it had been in 1290 and would not recover the pre-pandemic level until the 16th century.

QUARANTINE

In 1374 when another epidemic of the Black Death re-emerged in Europe, Venice instituted various public health controls such as isolating victims from healthy people and preventing ships with disease from landing at port. In 1377 the republic of Ragusa on the Adriatic Sea (now Dubrovnik in Yugoslavia) established a ships' landing station far from the city and harbor in which travelers suspected to have the plague had to spend thirty days, the *trentena*, to see whether they became ill and died or whether they remained healthy and could leave. The *trentena* was found to be too short and in 1403 in Venice, travelers from the Levant in the eastern Mediterranean were isolated in a hospital for forty days, the quarantena or quaranta giorni, from which we derive the term quarantine. This change to forty days may have also been related to other biblical and historical references such as the Christian observance of Lent, the period for which Christ fasted in the desert, or the ancient Greek doctrine of "critical days" which held that contagious disease will develop within 40 days after exposure. In the 14th and 15th centuries following, most countries in Europe had established quarantine, and in the 18th century, Habsburg established a cordon sanitaire, a line between infected and clean parts of the continent which ran from the Danube to the Balkans. It was manned by local peasants with checkpoints and quarantine stations to prevent infected people from crossing from eastern to western Europe.

In the 15th and 16th centuries, doctors wore a peculiar costume to protect themselves from the plague when they attended infected patients, first illustrated in a drawing by Paulus Furst in 1656 and later Jean-Jacques described a similar costume worn by the plague doctors at Nijmegen, an old Dutch town in Gelderland, in his 1721 work Treatise on the Plague. They wore a protective garb head to foot with leather or oilcloth robes, leggings, gloves and hood, a wide-brimmed hat which denoted their medical profession, and a beak-like mask with glass eyes and two breathing nostrils which was filled with aromatic herbs and flowers to ward off the miasmas. They avoided contact with patients by taking their pulse with a stick or issued prescriptions for aromatic herb inhalations passing them through the door, and buboes were lanced with knives several feet long.

Fig. 1.1 The Black Death

THE GREAT PLAGUE OF LONDON OF 1665-1666

Plague continued to occur in small epidemics throughout the world but a major outbreak of the pneumonic plague occurred in Europe and England from 1665 to 1666. The epidemic was described by Samuel Pepys in his diaries in 1665 and by Daniel Defoe in 1722 in his A Journal of a Plague Year. People were incarcerated in their homes, doors painted with a cross. The epidemic reached a peak in September 1665 when 7,000 people per week were dying in London alone. Between 1665 and 1666 a fifth of London's population died, some 100,000 people. The Great Fire of London in 1666 and the subsequent rebuilding of timber and thatch houses with brick and tile disturbed the rats' normal habitat and led to a reduction in their numbers, and may have been a contributing factor to the end of the epidemic.

An old English nursery rhyme published in Kate Greenaway's book Mother Goose 1881 reminds us of the symptoms of the plague :

'Ring, a-ring, o'rosies, (a red blistery rash)

A pocket full of posies (fragrant herbs and flowers to ward off the 'miasmas')

Atishoo, atishoo (the sneeze and the cough heralding pneumonia)

We all fall.' (all dead)

Plague waxed and waned in Europe until the late 18th century, but not with the virulence and mortality of the 14th century European Black Death.

THE THIRD PANDEMIC OF 1894

The plague re-emerged from its wild rodent reservoir in the remote Chinese province of Yunnan in 1855. From there the disease advanced along with the tin and opium routes and reached the provincial capital of Kunming in 1866, the Gulf of Tonkin in 1867, and the Kwangtung province port of Pakhoi (now Pei-hai) in 1882. In 1894 it had reached Canton and then spread to Hong Kong. It had spread to Bombay by 1896 and by 1900 had reached ports on every continent, carried by infected rats traveling the international trade routes on the new steamships. It was in Hong Kong in 1894 that Alexandre Yersin discovered the bacillus now known as Yersinia pestis, and in Karachi in 1898 that Paul-Louis Simond discovered the brown rat was the primary host and the rat flea the vector of the disease.

In 1900 the plague came to Australia where the first major outbreak occurred in Sydney, its epicenter at the Darling Harbour wharves, spreading to the city, Surry Hills, Glebe, Leichhardt, Redfern, and The Rocks, and causing 100 deaths. John Ashburton-Thompson, the chief medical officer, recorded the epidemic and confirmed that rats were the source and their fleas were the vectors in the epidemic. There were 12 major outbreaks of plague in Australia from 1900 to 1925 with 1371 cases and 535 deaths, most cases occurring in Sydney.

The third pandemic waxed and waned throughout the world for the next five decades and did not end until 1959, in that time plague had caused over 15 million deaths, the majority of which were in India. There have been outbreaks of plague since, such as in China and Tanzania in 1983, Zaire in 1992, and India, Mozambique, and Zimbabwe in 199415, 27. In Madagascar in the mid-1990s, a multi-drug resistant strain of the bacillus was identified15, 28. Currently, around 2,000 cases occur annually, mostly in Africa, Asia, and South America, with a global case fatality rate of 5% to 15%.

Bubonic plague is a virulent disease with a significant mortality rate, transmitted primarily by the bite of the rat flea or through person-to-person when in its pneumonic form. There have been innumerable epidemics of plague throughout history, but it was the pandemics of the 6th, 14th, and 20th centuries that have had the most impact on human society, not only in terms of the great mortalities but also the social, economic and cultural consequences that resulted. The course of development of communities and nations was altered several times. Much has changed to prevent the recurrence of the pandemic plagues, such as the development of the germ theory and the science of bacteriology, public health measures such as quarantine, and antibiotics such as streptomycin, but plague today is still an important and potentially serious threat to the health of people and animals.

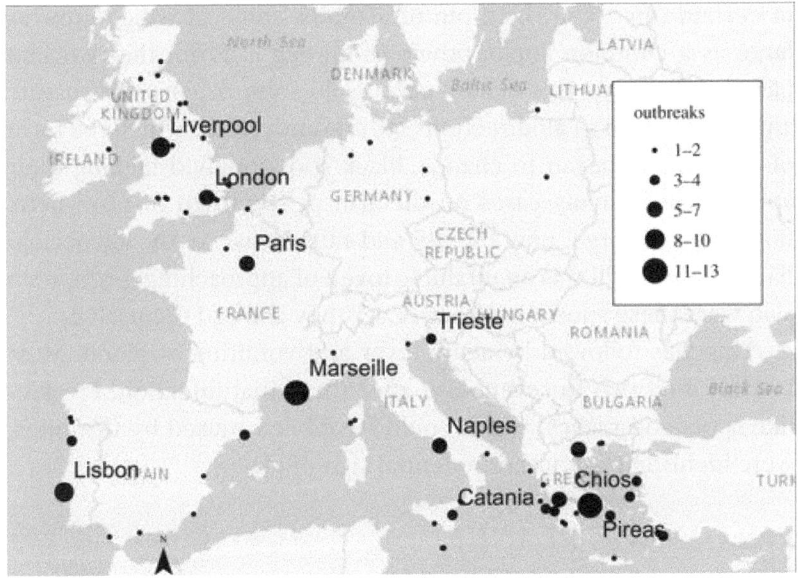

Fig. 1.2 The Third Plague Pandemic in Europe

SIGNS AND SYMPTOMS

BUBONIC PLAGUE

Symptoms of the disease include a fever of 38–41 °C (100–106 °F), headaches, painful aching joints, nausea and vomiting, and a general feeling of malaise. Left untreated, of those that contract the bubonic plague, 80 percent die within eight days.

Contemporary accounts of the pandemic are varied and often imprecise. The most commonly noted symptom was the appearance of buboes (or gavocciolos) in the groin, neck, and armpits, which oozed pus and bled when opened. Boccaccio's description:

In men and women alike it first betrayed itself by the emergence of certain tumors in the groin or armpits, some of which grew as large as a common apple, others as an egg ... From the two said parts of the body this deadly gavocciolo soon began to propagate and spread itself in all directions indifferently; after which the form of the malady began to change, black spots or livid making their appearance in many cases on the arm or the thigh or elsewhere, now few and large, now minute and numerous. As the gavocciolo had been and still was an infallible token of approaching death, such also were these spots on whomsoever they showed themselves.

This was followed by acute fever and vomiting of blood. Most victims died two to seven days after the initial infection. Freckle-like spots and rashes, which could have been caused by flea-bites, were identified as another potential sign of plague.

PNEUMONIC PLAGUE

The incubation period of pneumonic plague is usually just 1 to 3 days. Patients develop fever, headache, weakness, and rapidly developing pneumonia with shortness of breath, chest pain, cough, and sometimes bloody or watery mucous. Pneumonic plague may develop from inhaling infectious droplets or may develop from untreated bubonic or septicemic plague after the bacteria spread to the lungs. Pneumonia may cause respiratory failure and shock. Pneumonic plague is the most serious form of the disease and is the only form of plague that can be spread from person to person (by infectious droplets).

SEPTICEMIC PLAGUE

The incubation period of septicemic plague is poorly defined but likely occurs within days of exposure. Patients develop fever, chills, extreme weakness, abdominal pain, shock, and possibly bleeding into the skin and other organs. Skin and other tissues may turn black and die, especially on fingers, toes, and the nose. Septicemic plague can occur as the first symptom of plague or may develop from untreated bubonic plague. This form results from bites of infected fleas or from handling an infected animal.

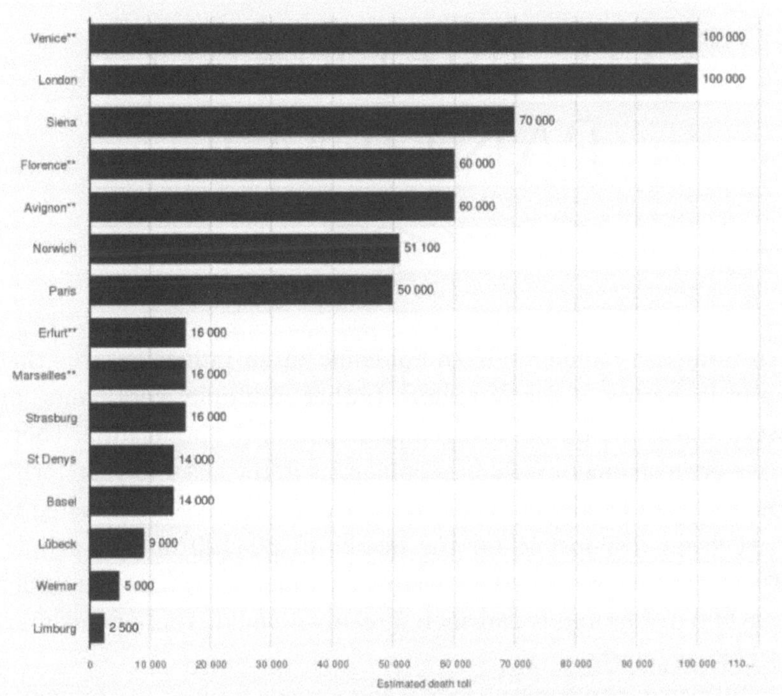

Fig. 1.3 Estimated Death Toll in European Cities

CHAPTER TWO

THE INFLUENZA PANDEMIC

An influenza pandemic is an epidemic of an influenza virus that spreads across a large region (either multiple continents or worldwide) and infects a large proportion of the population. There have been six major influenza epidemics in the last 140 years, with the 1918 flu pandemic being the most severe; this is estimated to have been responsible for the deaths of 50–100 million people. The most recent, the 2009 swine flu pandemic, resulted in under 300,000 deaths and is considered relatively mild. These pandemics occur irregularly.

Influenza pandemics occur when a new strain of the influenza virus is transmitted to humans from another animal species. Species that are thought to be important in the emergence of new human strains are pigs, chickens, and ducks. These novel strains are unaffected by any immunity people may have to older strains of human influenza and can therefore spread extremely rapidly and infect very large numbers of people. Influenza A viruses can occasionally be transmitted from wild birds to other species, causing outbreaks in domestic poultry, and may give rise to human influenza pandemics. The propagation of influenza viruses throughout the world is thought in part to be by bird migrations, though commercial shipments of live bird products might also be implicated, as well as human travel patterns.

The World Health Organization (WHO) has produced a six-stage classification that describes the process by which a novel influenza virus moves from the first few infections in humans through to a pandemic. This starts with the virus mostly infecting animals, with a few cases where animals infect people, then moves through the stage where the virus begins to spread directly between people and ends with a pandemic when infections from the new virus have spread worldwide.

One strain of virus that may produce a pandemic in the future is a highly pathogenic variation of the H5N1 subtype of the influenza A virus. On 11 June 2009, a new strain of H1N1 influenza was declared to be a pandemic (Stage 6) by the WHO after evidence of spreading in the southern hemisphere. The 13 November 2009 worldwide update by the WHO stated that "as of 8 November 2009, worldwide more than 206 countries and overseas territories or communities have reported [503,536] laboratory-confirmed cases of pandemic influenza H1N1 2009, including over 6,250 deaths."

Influenza, commonly known as the flu, is an infectious disease in birds and mammals. It was thought to be caused by comets, earthquakes, volcanoes, cosmic dust, the rising and setting of the sun, vapors arising from the air and ground, or a blast from the stars. Now we know that it is caused by an RNA virus of the family Orthomyxoviridae (the influenza viruses). In humans, common symptoms of influenza infection are fever, sore throat, muscle pains, severe headache, coughing, weakness, and fatigue. In more serious cases, influenza causes pneumonia, which can be fatal, particularly in young children and the elderly. While sometimes confused with the common cold, influenza is a much more severe disease and is caused by a different type of virus. Although nausea and vomiting can be produced, especially in children, these symptoms are more characteristic of unrelated gastroenteritis, which is sometimes called "stomach flu" or "24-hour flu."

Typically, influenza is transmitted from infected mammals through the air by coughs or sneezes, creating aerosols containing the virus, and from infected birds through their droppings.

Influenza can also be transmitted by saliva, nasal secretions, feces, and blood. Healthy individuals can become infected if they breathe in a virus-laden aerosol directly, or if they touch their eyes, nose, or mouth after touching any of the aforementioned bodily fluids (or surfaces contaminated with those fluids). Flu viruses can remain infectious for about one week at human body temperature, over 30 days at 0 °C (32 °F), and indefinitely at very low temperatures (such as lakes in northeast Siberia). Most influenza strains can be inactivated easily by disinfectants and detergents.

Flu spreads around the world in seasonal epidemics. Ten pandemics were recorded before the Spanish flu of 1918. Three influenza pandemics occurred during the 20th century and killed tens of millions of people, with each of these pandemics being caused by the appearance of a new strain of the virus in humans. Often, these new strains result from the spread of an existing flu virus to humans from other animal species, so proximity between humans and animals can promote epidemics. In addition, epidemiological factors, such as the WWI practice of packing soldiers with severe influenza illness into field hospitals while soldiers with mild illness stayed outside on the battlefield, are an important determinant of whether or not a new strain of influenza virus will spur a pandemic. (During the 1918 Spanish flu pandemic, this practice served to promote the evolution of more virulent viral strains over those that produced mild illness.) When it first killed humans in Asia in the 1990s, a deadly avian strain of H5N1 posed a great risk for a new influenza pandemic; however, this virus did not mutate to spread easily between people.

Vaccinations against influenza are most commonly given to high-risk humans in industrialized countries and farmed poultry. The most common human vaccine is the trivalent influenza vaccine that contains purified and inactivated material from three viral strains. Typically this vaccine includes material from two influenza A virus subtypes and one influenza B virus strain. A vaccine formulated for one year may be ineffective in the following year since the influenza virus changes rapidly over time and different strains become dominant. Antiviral drugs can be used to treat influenza, with neuraminidase inhibitors being particularly effective.

TYPES OF VIRUS

Influenza viruses comprise four species. Each of the four species is the sole member of its own genus, and the four influenza genera comprise four of the seven genera in the family Orthomyxoviridae. They are:

Influenza A virus (IAV), genus Alphainfluenzavirus

Influenza B virus (IBV), genus Betainfluenzavirus

Influenza C virus (ICV), genus Gammainfluenzavirus

Influenza D virus (IDV), genus Deltainfluenzavirus

IAV is responsible for most cases of severe illness as well as seasonal epidemics and occasional pandemics. It infects people of all ages but tends to disproportionately cause severe illness in the elderly, the very young, and those who have chronic health issues. Birds are the primary reservoir of IAV, especially aquatic birds such as ducks, geese, shorebirds, and gulls, but the virus also circulates among mammals, including pigs, horses, and marine mammals. IAV is classified into subtypes based on the viral proteins haemagglutinin (H) and neuraminidase (N). As of 2019, 18 H subtypes and 11 N subtypes have been identified. Most potential combinations have been reported in birds, but H17-18 and N10-11 have only been found in bats. Only H subtypes H1-3 and N subtypes N1-2 are known to have circulated in humans, the current IAV subtypes in circulation being H1N1 and H3N2. IAVs can be classified more specifically to also include natural host species, geographical origin, year of isolation, and strain number, such as H1N1/A/duck/Alberta/35/76.

IBV mainly infects humans but has been identified in seals, horses, dogs, and pigs. IBV does not have subtypes like IAV but has two antigenically distinct lineages, termed the B/Victoria/2/1987-like and B/Yamagata/16/1988-like lineages, or simply

(B/)Victoria(-like) and (B/)Yamagata(-like). Both lineages are in circulation in humans, disproportionately affecting children. IBVs contribute to seasonal epidemics alongside IAVs but have never been associated with a pandemic.

ICV, like IBV, is primarily found in humans, though it also has been detected in pigs, feral dogs, dromedary camels, cattle, and dogs. ICV infection primarily affects children and is usually asymptomatic or has mild cold-like symptoms, though more severe symptoms such as gastroenteritis and pneumonia can occur. Unlike IAV and IBV, ICV has not been a major focus of research pertaining to antiviral drugs, vaccines, and other measures against influenza. ICV is subclassified into six genetic/antigenic lineages.

IDV has been isolated from pigs and cattle, the latter being the natural reservoir. The infection has also been observed in humans, horses, dromedary camels, and small ruminants such as goats and sheep. IDV is distantly related to ICV. While cattle workers have occasionally tested positive for prior IDV infection, it is not known to cause disease in humans. ICV and IDV experience a slower rate of antigenic evolution than IAV and IBV. Because of this antigenic stability, relatively few novel lineages emerge.

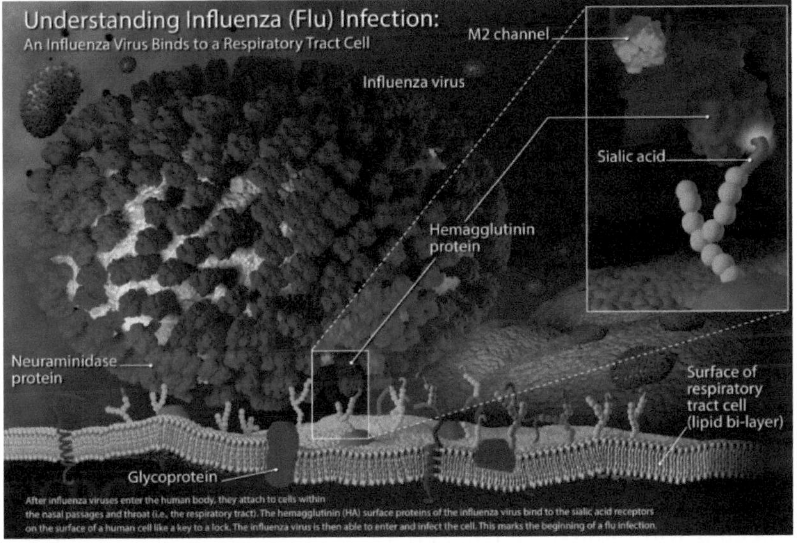

Fig. 2.1 Structure of Influenza Virus

VARIANTS AND SUBTYPES OF INFLUENZA VIRUS A

Variants of Influenzavirus A are identified and named according to the isolate that they are like and thus are presumed to share lineage (for example Fujian flu virus); according to their typical host (example Human flu virus); according to their subtype (example H3N2); and according to their deadliness (e.g., Low Pathogenic as discussed below). So flu from a virus similar to the isolate A/Fujian/411/2002(H3N2) is called Fujian flu, human flu, and H3N2 flu.

Variants are sometimes named according to the species (host) the strain is endemic in or adapted to. Some variants named using this convention are:

AVIAN INFLUENZA (BIRD FLU)

Avian influenza, known informally as avian flu or bird flu, is a variety of influenza caused by viruses adapted to birds. The type with the greatest risk is highly pathogenic avian influenza (HPAI). Bird flu is similar to swine flu, dog flu, horse flu, and human flu as an illness caused by strains of influenza viruses that have adapted to a specific host. Out of the three types of influenza viruses (A, B, and C), influenza A virus is a zoonotic infection with a natural reservoir almost entirely in birds. Avian influenza, for most purposes, refers to the influenza A virus.

Though influenza A is adapted to birds, it can also stably adapt and sustain person-to-person transmission. Recent influenza research into the genes of the Spanish flu virus shows it to have genes adapted from both human and avian strains. Pigs can also be infected with human, avian, and swine influenza viruses, allowing for mixtures of genes (reassortment) to create a new virus, which can cause an antigenic shift to a new influenza A virus subtype which most people have little to no immune protection against.

Avian influenza strains are divided into two types based on their pathogenicity: high pathogenicity (HP) or low pathogenicity (LP). The most well-known HPAI strain, H5N1, was first isolated from a farmed goose in Guangdong Province, China in 1996, and also has low pathogenic strains found in North America. Companion birds in captivity are unlikely to contract the virus and there has been no report of a companion bird with avian influenza since 2003. Pigeons can contract avian strains, but rarely become ill and are incapable of transmitting the virus efficiently to humans or other animals.

Between early 2013 and early 2017, 916 lab-confirmed human cases of H7N9 were reported to the World Health Organization (WHO). On 9 January 2017, the National Health and Family Planning Commission of China reported to WHO 106 cases of H7N9 which occurred from late November through late December, including 35 deaths, 2 potential cases of human-to-human transmission, and 80 of these 106 persons stating that they have visited live poultry markets. The cases are reported from Jiangsu, Zhejiang, Anhui, Guangdong, Shanghai, Fujian and Hunan. Similar sudden increases in the number of human cases of H7N9 have occurred in previous years during December and January.

Genetic factors in distinguishing between "human flu viruses" and "avian flu viruses" include:

PB2 (RNA polymerase)-

Amino acid (or residue) position 627 in the PB2 protein encoded by the PB2 RNA gene. Until H5N1, all known avian influenza viruses had a Glu at position 627, while all human influenza viruses had a Lys.

HA (hemagglutinin)-

Avian influenza HA viruses bind alpha 2-3 sialic acid receptors, while human influenza HA viruses bind alpha 2-6 sialic acid receptors. Swine influenza viruses can bind both types of sialic acid receptors. Hemagglutinin is the major antigen of the virus against which neutralizing antibodies are produced, and influenza virus epidemics are associated with changes in its antigenic structure. This was originally derived from pigs, and should technically be referred to as "pig flu".

The evolution of the avian influenza virus has been influenced by genetic variation in the virus population due to genome segment reassortment and mutation. Also, homologous recombination occurs in viral genes, suggesting that genetic variation generated by homologous recombination has also played a role in driving the evolution of the virus and potentially has affected virulence and the host range.

Avian influenza is most often spread by contact between infected and healthy birds, though can also be spread indirectly through contaminated equipment. The virus is found in secretions from the nostrils, mouth, and eyes of infected birds as well as their droppings. HPAI infection is spread to people often through direct contact with infected poultry, such as during slaughter or plucking. Though the virus can spread through airborne secretions, the disease itself is not airborne. Highly pathogenic strains spread quickly among flocks and can destroy a flock within 28 hours; the less pathogenic strains may affect egg production but are much less deadly.

Although humans can contract the avian influenza virus from birds, human-to-human contact is much more difficult without prolonged contact. However, public health officials are concerned that strains of avian flu may mutate to become easily transmissible between humans. Some strains of avian influenza are present in the intestinal tract of large numbers of shorebirds and water birds, but these strains rarely cause human infection.

Five manmade ecosystems have contributed to modern avian influenza virus ecology: integrated indoor commercial poultry, range-raised commercial poultry, live poultry markets, backyard and hobby flocks, and bird collection and trading systems including cockfighting. Indoor commercial poultry has had the largest impact on the spread of HPAI, with the increase in HPAI outbreaks largely the result of increased commercial production since the 1990s.

In the early days of the HPAI H5N1 pandemic, village poultry and their owners were frequently implicated in disease transmission. Village poultry, also known as backyard and hobby flocks, are small flocks raised under extensive conditions and often allowed free range between multiple households. However, research has shown that these flocks pose less of a threat than intensively raised commercial poultry with homogenous genetic stock and poor biosecurity. The backyard and village poultry also do not travel great distances compared to the transport of intensively raised poultry and contribute less to the spread of HPAI. This initial implication of Asian poultry farmers as one broad category presented challenges to prevention recommendations as commercial strategies did not necessarily apply to backyard poultry flocks.

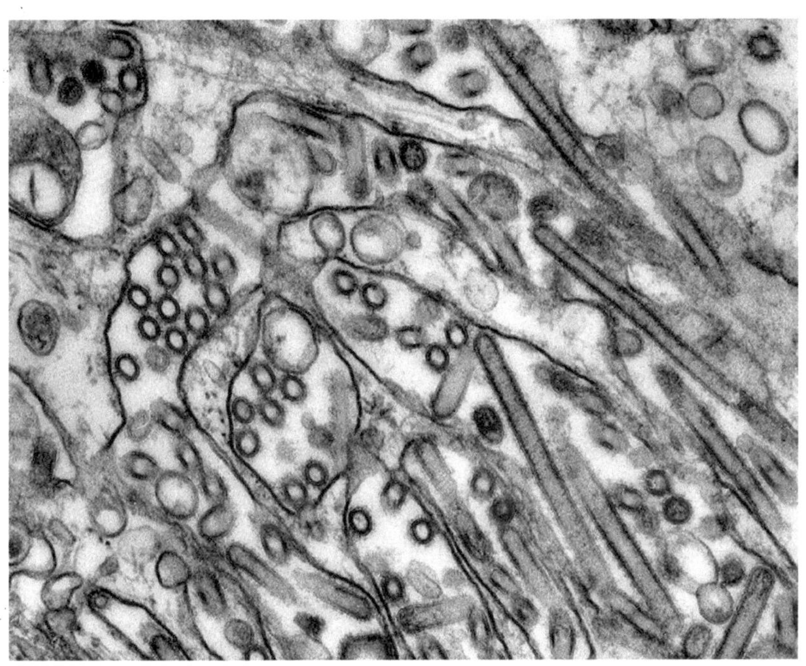

Fig. 2.2 H5N1 (Avian Influenza)

CANINE INFLUENZA (DOG FLU)

Canine influenza (dog flu) is influenza occurring in canine animals. Canine influenza is caused by varieties of influenza virus A, such as equine influenza virus H3N8, which was discovered to cause disease in canines in 2004. Because of the lack of previous exposure to this virus, dogs have no natural immunity to it. Therefore, the disease is rapidly transmitted between individual dogs. Canine influenza may be endemic in some regional dog populations of the United States. It is a disease with high morbidity (incidence of symptoms) but a low incidence of death.

A newer form was identified in Asia during the 2000s and has since caused outbreaks in the US as well. It is a mutation of H3N2 that adapted from its avian influenza origins. Vaccines have been developed for both strains.

The highly contagious equine influenza A virus subtype H3N8 was found to have been the cause of Greyhound race dog fatalities from a respiratory illness at a Florida racetrack in January 2004. The exposure and transfer occurred at horse-racing tracks, where dog racing had also occurred. This was the first evidence of an influenza A virus causing disease in dogs. However, serum collected from racing Greyhounds between 1984 and 2004 and tested for canine influenza virus (CIV) in 2007 had positive tests going as far back as 1999. CIV possibly caused some of the respiratory disease outbreaks at tracks between 1999 and 2003.

H3N8 was also responsible for a major dog-flu outbreak in New York state in all breeds of dogs. From January to May 2005, outbreaks occurred at 20 racetracks in 10 states (Arizona, Arkansas, Colorado, Florida, Iowa, Kansas, Massachusetts, Rhode Island, Texas, and West Virginia). As of August 2006, dog flu has been confirmed in 22 U.S. states, including pet dogs in Wyoming, California, Connecticut, Delaware, and Hawaii. Three areas in the United States may now be considered endemic for CIV due to continuous waves of cases: New York, southern Florida, and northern Colorado/southern Wyoming. No evidence shows the virus can be transferred to people, cats, or other species.

H5N1 (avian influenza) was also shown to cause death in one dog in Thailand, following ingestion of an infected duck.

The H3N2 virus made its first appearance in Canada at the start of 2018, following the importation of two unknowingly infected canines from South Korea. Following this incidence, reports of the virus possibly spreading, with two other canines reporting alarming symptoms, were made public. By March 5th, 25 cases of infection were reportedly spread, although the number is thought to be closer to approximately 100.

Influenza A viruses are enveloped, negative-sense, single-stranded RNA viruses. Genome analysis has shown that H3N8 was transferred from horses to dogs and then adapted to dogs through point mutations in the genes. The incubation period is two to five days, and viral shedding may occur for seven to ten days following the onset of symptoms. It does not induce a persistent carrier state.

About 80% of infected dogs with H3N8 show symptoms, usually mild (the other 20% have subclinical infections), and the fatality rate for Greyhounds in early outbreaks was 5% to 8%, although the overall fatality rate in the general pet and shelter population is probably less than 1%. Symptoms of the mild form include a cough that lasts for 10 to 30 days and possibly a greenish nasal discharge. Dogs with the more severe form may have a high fever and pneumonia. Pneumonia in these dogs is not caused by the influenza virus, but by secondary bacterial infections. The fatality rate of dogs that develop pneumonia secondary to canine influenza can reach 50% if not given proper treatment. Necropsies in dogs that die from the disease have revealed severe hemorrhagic pneumonia and evidence of vasculitis.

EQUINE INFLUENZA (HORSE FLU)

Equine influenza (horse flu) is the disease caused by strains of influenza A that are enzootic in horse species. Equine influenza occurs globally, previously caused by two main strains of the virus: equine-1 (H7N7) and equine-2 (H3N8). The OIE now considers H7N7 strains likely to be extinct since these strains have not been isolated for over 20 years. Predominant international circulating H3N8 strains are Florida sublineages of the American lineage; clade 1 predominates in the Americas and clade 2 in Europe. (Elton and Cullinane, 2013; Paillot, 2014; Slater et al., 2013). The disease has a nearly 100% infection rate in an unvaccinated horse population with no prior exposure to the virus.

While equine influenza is historically not known to affect humans, impacts of past outbreaks have been devastating due to the economic reliance on horses for communication (postal service), military (cavalry), and general transportation. In modern times, though, the ramifications of equine influenza are most clear in the horse-racing industry.

Equine influenza is characterized by a very high rate of transmission among horses and has a relatively short incubation time of one to three days. Clinical signs of equine influenza include fever (up to 106 °F [41 °C]), nasal discharge, have a dry, hacking cough, depression, loss of appetite, and weakness. Secondary infections may include pneumonia. Horses that are mildly affected will recover within 2 to 3 weeks; however, it may take up to 6 months for recovery for severely affected horses. Horses that become immune may not show signs but will still shed the virus.

An 1872 report on equine influenza describes the disease as:

"An epizootic specific fever of a very debilitating type, with inflammation of the respiratory mucous membrane, and less frequently of other organs, having an average duration of ten to fifteen days, and not conferring immunity from the second attack in subsequent epizootics."

— James Law, Report of the Commissioner of Agriculture for the year 1872.

Equine influenza is caused by several strains of the influenza A virus endemic to horses. Viruses that cause equine influenza were first isolated in 1956. The equine-1 virus affects the heart muscle, while the equine-2 virus is much more severe and systemic. The virus is spread by infected, coughing horses in addition to contaminated buckets, brushes, tack, and other stable equipment. The influenza virus causes symptoms by replicating within respiratory epithelial cells, destroying tracheal and bronchial epithelium and cilia.

When horse contracts the equine influenza virus, rest and supportive care are advised so that complications do not occur. Veterinarians recommend at least one week of rest for every day that the fever persists with a minimum of three days' rest. This allows the damaged mucociliary apparatus to regenerate. Non-steroidal anti-inflammatory drugs are administered if the fever reaches greater than 104 °F (40 °C). If complications occur, such as the onset of pneumonia, or if the fever lasts more than 3 to 4 days, antibiotics are often administered.

An epizootic outbreak of equine influenza during 1872 in North America became known as "The Great Epizootic of 1872". The outbreak is known as the "most destructive recorded episode of equine influenza in history". In 1870, three-fourths of Americans lived in rural areas (towns under 2,500 population, and farms). Horse and mule power was used for moving wagons and carriages, and pulling plows and farm equipment. The census of 1870 counted 7.1 million horses and 1.1 million mules, as well as 39 million humans. With most urban horses and mules incapacitated for a week or two, humans used wheelbarrows and pulled the wagons. About 1% of the animals died, and the rest fully recovered.

The first cases of the disease were reported from Ontario, Canada. By October 1, 1872, the first case occurred in Toronto. All the streetcar horses and major livery stables were affected within only three days. By the middle of October, the disease had reached Montreal, Detroit, and New England. On October 25, 1872, The New York Times reported on the extent of the outbreak, claiming that nearly all public stables in the city had been affected and that the majority of the horses owned in the private sector had essentially been rendered useless to their owners. Only days later, the Times went on to report that 95% of all horses in Rochester, New York, had been affected, while the disease was also making its way quickly through the state of Maine and had already affected all fire horses in the city of Providence, Rhode Island.

On October 30, 1872, The New York Times reported that a complete suspension of travel had been noted in the state. The same report also took note of massive freight backups being caused by the lack of transportation ability that was arising as a result of the outbreak. Cities such as Buffalo and New York were left without effective ways to move merchandise through the streets, and even the Erie Canal was left with boats full of goods idling in its waters because they were pulled by horses. By November, many states were reporting cases. The street railway industry ground to a halt in late 1872.

Boston was hard hit by a major fire downtown on November 9 as firemen pulled the necessary firefighting equipment by hand. The city commission investigating the fire found that fire crews' response times were delayed by only a matter of minutes. The city then began to buy steam-powered equipment.

In New York, 7,000 of the city's approximately 11,000 horses fell ill, and mortality rates ranged between 1.0% and 10%. Many horses were unable to stand in their stalls; those that could stand coughed violently and were too weak to pull any loads or support riders. The vast majority of affected horses that survived were back to full health by the following spring.

HUMAN INFLUENZA

Influenza, commonly known as "the flu", is an infectious disease caused by influenza viruses. Symptoms range from mild to severe and often include fever, runny nose, sore throat, muscle pain, headache, coughing, and fatigue. These symptoms begin from one to four days after exposure to the virus (typically two days) and last for about 2–8 days. Diarrhea and vomiting can occur, particularly in children. Influenza may progress to pneumonia, which can be caused by the virus or by a subsequent bacterial infection. Other complications of infection include acute respiratory distress syndrome, meningitis, encephalitis, and worsening of pre-existing health problems such as asthma and cardiovascular disease.

There are four types of influenza virus, termed influenza viruses A, B, C, and D. Aquatic birds are the primary source of the Influenza A virus (IAV), which is also widespread in various mammals, including humans and pigs. Influenza B virus (IBV) and Influenza C virus (ICV) primarily infect humans, and Influenza D virus (IDV) is found in cattle and pigs. IAV and IBV circulate in humans and cause seasonal epidemics, and ICV causes a mild infection, primarily in children. IDV can infect humans but is not known to cause illness. In humans, influenza viruses are primarily transmitted through respiratory droplets produced from coughing and sneezing.

Transmission through aerosols and intermediate objects and surfaces contaminated by the virus also occur.

Frequent hand washing and covering one's mouth and nose when coughing and sneezing reduce transmission. Annual vaccination can help to provide protection against influenza. Influenza viruses, particularly IAV, evolve quickly, so flu vaccines are updated regularly to match which influenza strains are in circulation. Vaccines currently in use provide protection against IAV subtypes H1N1 and H3N2 and one or two IBV subtypes. Influenza infection is diagnosed with laboratory methods such as antibody or antigen tests and a polymerase chain reaction (PCR) to identify viral nucleic acid. The disease can be treated with supportive measures and, in severe cases, with antiviral drugs such as oseltamivir. In healthy individuals, influenza is typically self-limiting and rarely fatal, but it can be deadly in high-risk groups.

In a typical year, 5–15% of the population contracts influenza. There are 3–5 million severe cases annually, with up to 650,000 respiratory-related deaths globally each year. Deaths most commonly occur in high-risk groups, including young children, the elderly, and people with chronic health conditions. In temperate regions of the world, the number of influenza cases peaks during winter, whereas in the tropics influenza can occur year-round. Since the late 1800s, large outbreaks of novel influenza strains that spread globally, called pandemics, have occurred every 10–50 years. Five flu pandemics have occurred since 1900: the Spanish flu in 1918–1920, which was the most severe flu pandemic, the Asian flu in 1957, the Hong Kong flu in 1968, the Russian flu in 1977, and the swine flu pandemic in 2009.

The time between exposure to the virus and the development of symptoms, called the incubation period, is 1–4 days, most commonly 1–2 days. Many infections, however, are asymptomatic. The onset of symptoms is sudden, and initial symptoms are predominately non-specific, including fever, chills, headaches, muscle pain or aching, a feeling of discomfort, loss of appetite, lack of energy/fatigue, and confusion. These symptoms are usually accompanied by respiratory symptoms such as a dry cough, sore or dry throat, hoarse voice, and a stuffy or runny nose. Coughing is the most common symptom. Gastrointestinal symptoms may also occur, including nausea, vomiting, diarrhea, and gastroenteritis, especially in children. The standard influenza symptoms typically last for 2–8 days. A 2021 study suggests influenza can cause long-lasting symptoms in a similar way to long COVID.

Symptomatic infections are usually mild and limited to the upper respiratory tract, but progression to pneumonia is relatively common. Pneumonia may be caused by the primary viral infection or by a secondary bacterial infection. Primary pneumonia is characterized by rapid progression of fever, cough, labored breathing, and low oxygen levels that cause bluish skin. It is especially common among those who have an underlying cardiovascular disease such as rheumatic heart disease. Secondary pneumonia typically has a period of improvement in symptoms for 1–3 weeks followed by recurrent fever, sputum production, and fluid buildup in the lungs, but can also occur just a few days after influenza symptoms appear. About a third of primary pneumonia cases are followed by secondary pneumonia, which is most frequently caused by the bacteria Streptococcus pneumoniae and Staphylococcus aureus.

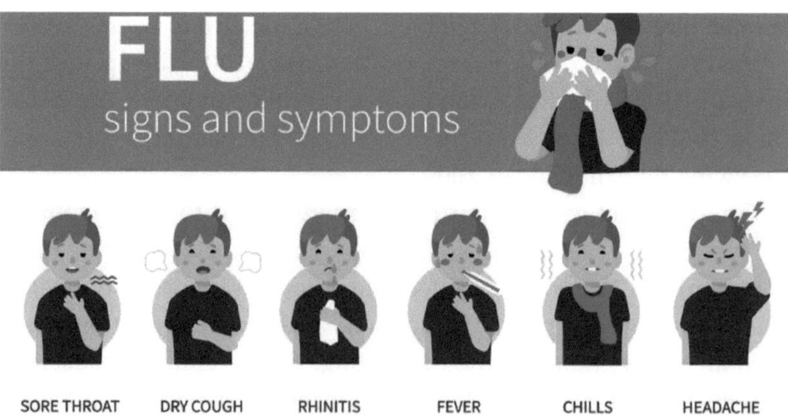

Fig. 2.3 Symptoms of Influenza

GENOME

Influenza viruses have a negative-sense, single-stranded RNA genome that is segmented. The negative sense of the genome means it can be used as a template to synthesize messenger RNA (mRNA). IAV and IBV have eight genome segments that encode 10 major proteins. ICV and IDV have seven genome segments that encode nine major proteins. Three segments encode three subunits of an RNA-dependent RNA polymerase (RdRp) complex: PB1, a transcriptase, PB2, which recognizes 5' caps, and PA (P3 for ICV and IDV), an endonuclease. The matrix protein (M1) and membrane protein (M2) share a segment, as do the non-structural protein (NS1) and the nuclear export protein (NEP). For IAV and IBV, hemagglutinin (HA) and neuraminidase (NA) are encoded on one segment each, whereas ICV and IDV encode a hemagglutinin-esterase fusion (HEF) protein on one segment that merges the functions of HA and NA. The final genome segment encodes the viral nucleoprotein (NP). Influenza viruses also encode various accessory proteins, such as PB1-F2 and PA-X, that are expressed through alternative open reading frames and which are important in host defense suppression, virulence, and pathogenicity.

The virus particle, called a virion, is pleomorphic and varies between being filamentous, bacilliform, or spherical in shape. Clinical isolates tend to be pleomorphic, whereas strains adapted to laboratory growth typically produce spherical virions. Filamentous virions are about 250 nanometers (nm) by 80 nm, bacilliform 120–250 by 95 nm, and spherical 120 nm in diameter. The virion consists of each segment of the genome bound to nucleoproteins in separate ribonucleoprotein (RNP) complexes for each segment, all of which are surrounded by a lipid bilayer membrane called the viral envelope. There is a copy of the RdRp, all subunits included, bound to each RNP. The envelope is reinforced structurally by matrix proteins on the interior that encloses the RNPs, and the envelope contains HA and NA (or HEF) proteins extending outward from the exterior surface of the envelope. HA and HEF proteins have distinct "head" and "stalk" structures. M2 proteins form proton ion channels through the viral envelope that are required for viral entry and exit. IBVs contain a surface protein named NB that is anchored in the envelope, but its function is unknown.

LIFE CYCLE

The viral life cycle begins by binding to a target cell. Binding is mediated by the viral HA proteins on the surface of the envelope, which binds to cells that contain sialic acid receptors on the surface of the cell membrane. For N1 subtypes with the "G147R" mutation and N2 subtypes, the NA protein can initiate entry. Prior to binding, NA proteins promote access to target cells by degrading mucous, which helps to remove extracellular decoy receptors that would impede access to target cells. After binding, the virus is internalized into the cell by an endosome that contains the virion inside it. The endosome is acidified by cellular vATPase to have lower pH, which triggers a conformational change in HA that allows fusion of the viral envelope with the endosomal membrane. At the same time, hydrogen ions diffuse into the virion through M2 ion channels, disrupting internal protein-protein interactions to release RNPs into the host cell's cytosol. The M1 protein shell surrounding RNPs is degraded, fully uncoating RNPs in the cytosol.

RNPs are then imported into the nucleus with the help of viral localization signals. There, the viral RNA polymerase transcribes mRNA using the genomic negative-sense strand as a template. The polymerase snatches 5' caps for viral mRNA from cellular RNA to prime mRNA synthesis and the 3'-end of mRNA is polyadenylated at the end of transcription. Once viral mRNA is transcribed, it is exported out of the nucleus and translated by host ribosomes in a cap-dependent manner to synthesize viral proteins. RdRp also synthesizes complementary positive-sense strands of the viral genome in a complementary RNP complex which are then used as templates by viral polymerases to synthesize copies of the negative-sense genome. During these processes, RdRps of avian influenza viruses (AIVs) function optimally at a higher temperature than mammalian influenza viruses.

Newly synthesized viral polymerase subunits and NP proteins are imported to the nucleus to further increase the rate of viral replication and form RNPs. HA, NA and M2 proteins are trafficked with the aid of M1 and NEP proteins to the cell membrane through the Golgi apparatus and inserted into the cell's membrane. Viral non-structural proteins including NS1, PB1-F2, and PA-X regulate host cellular processes to disable antiviral responses. PB1-F2 also interacts with PB1 to keep polymerases in the nucleus longer. M1 and NEP proteins localize to the nucleus during the later stages of infection, bind to viral RNPs, and mediate their export to the cytoplasm where they migrate to the cell membrane with the aid of recycled endosomes and are bundled into the segments of the genome.

Pyrogenic viruses leave the cell by budding from the cell membrane, which is initiated by the accumulation of M1 proteins at the cytoplasmic side of the membrane. The viral genome is incorporated inside a viral envelope derived from portions of the cell membrane that have HA, NA, and M2 proteins. At the end of budding, HA proteins remain attached to cellular sialic acid until they are cleaved by the sialidase activity of NA proteins. The virion is then released from the cell. The sialidase activity of NA also cleaves any sialic acid residues from the viral surface, which helps prevent newly assembled viruses from aggregating near the cell surface and improving infectivity. Similar to other aspects of influenza replication, optimal NA activity is temperature- and pH-dependent. Ultimately, the presence of large quantities of viral RNA in the cell triggers apoptosis, i.e. programmed cell death, which is initiated by cellular factors to restrict viral replication.

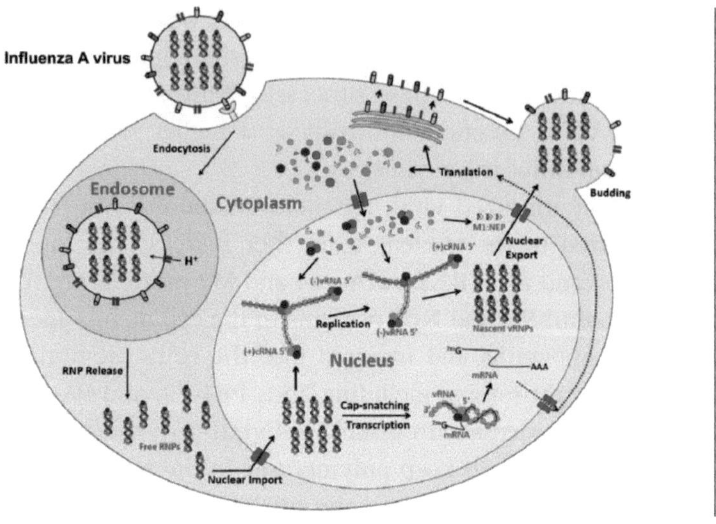

Fig. 2.4 Host Cell Invasion & Replication

ANTIGENIC DRIFT AND SHIFT

Two key processes that influenza viruses evolve through are antigenic drift and antigenic shift. Antigenic drift is when an influenza virus's antigens change due to the gradual accumulation of mutations in the antigen's (HA or NA) gene. This can occur in response to evolutionary pressure exerted by the host immune response. Antigenic drift is especially common for the HA protein, in which just a few amino acid changes in the head region can constitute antigenic drift. The result is the production of novel strains that can evade pre-existing antibody-mediated immunity. Antigenic drift occurs in all influenza species but is slower in B than A and slowest in C and D. Antigenic drift is a major cause of seasonal influenza, and requires that flu vaccines be updated annually. HA is the main component of inactivated vaccines, so surveillance monitors antigenic drift of this antigen among circulating strains. The antigenic evolution of influenza viruses in humans appears to be faster than influenza viruses in swine and equines. In wild birds, within-subtype antigenic variation appears to be limited but has been observed in poultry.

Antigenic shift is a sudden, drastic change in an influenza virus's antigen, usually HA. During the antigenic shift, antigenically different strains that infect the same cell can reassort genome segments with each other, producing hybrid progeny. Since all influenza viruses have segmented genomes, all are capable of reassortment. Antigenic shift, however, only occurs among influenza viruses of the same genus and most commonly occurs among IAVs. In particular, reassortment is very common in AIVs, creating a large diversity of influenza viruses in birds, but is uncommon in human, equine, and canine lineages. Pigs, bats, and quails have receptors for both mammalian and avian IAVs, so they are potential "mixing vessels" for reassortment. If an animal strain reassorts with a human strain, then a novel strain can emerge that is capable of human-to-human transmission. This has caused pandemics, but only a limited number have occurred, so it is difficult to predict when the next will happen.

TRANSMISSION

People who are infected can transmit influenza viruses through breathing, talking, coughing, and sneezing, which spread respiratory droplets and aerosols that contain virus particles into the air. A person susceptible to infection can then contract influenza by coming into contact with these particles. Respiratory droplets are relatively large and travel less than two meters before falling onto nearby surfaces. Aerosols are smaller and remain suspended in the air longer, so they take longer to settle and can travel further than respiratory droplets. Inhalation of aerosols can lead to infection, but most transmission is in the area about two meters around an infected person via respiratory droplets that come into contact with the mucosa of the upper respiratory tract.

Transmission through contact with a person, bodily fluids, or intermediate objects (fomites) can also occur, such as through contaminated hands and surfaces since influenza viruses can survive for hours on non-porous surfaces. If one's hands are contaminated, then touching one's face can cause infection.

Influenza is usually transmissible from one day before the onset of symptoms to 5–7 days after. In healthy adults, the virus is shed for up to 3–5 days. In children and the immunocompromised, the virus may be transmissible for several weeks. Children ages 2–17 are considered to be the primary and most efficient spreaders of influenza. Children who have not had multiple prior exposures to influenza viruses shed the virus in greater quantities and for a longer duration than other children. People who are at risk of exposure to influenza include health care workers, social care workers, and those who live with or care for people vulnerable to influenza. In long-term care facilities, the flu can spread rapidly after it is introduced. A variety of factors likely encourage influenza transmission, including lower temperature, lower absolute and relative humidity, less ultraviolet radiation from the Sun, and crowding. Influenza viruses that infect the upper respiratory tract like H1N1 tend to be milder but more transmissible, whereas those that infect the lower respiratory tract like H5N1 tend to cause more severe illness but are less contagious.

PATHOPHYSIOLOGY

In humans, influenza viruses first cause infection by infecting epithelial cells in the respiratory tract. Illness during infection is primarily the result of lung inflammation and compromise caused by epithelial cell infection and death, combined with inflammation caused by the immune system's response to infection. Non-respiratory organs can become involved, but the mechanisms by which influenza is involved in these cases are unknown. Severe respiratory illness can be caused by multiple, non-exclusive mechanisms, including obstruction of the airways, loss of alveolar structure, loss of lung epithelial integrity due to epithelial cell infection and death, and degradation of the extracellular matrix that maintains lung structure. In particular, alveolar cell infection appears to drive severe symptoms since this results in impaired gas exchange and enables viruses to infect endothelial cells, which produce large quantities of pro-inflammatory cytokines.

Pneumonia caused by influenza viruses is characterized by high levels of viral replication in the lower respiratory tract, accompanied by a strong pro-inflammatory response called a cytokine storm. Infection with H5N1 or H7N9 especially produces high levels of pro-inflammatory cytokines. In bacterial infections, early depletion of macrophages during influenza creates a favorable environment in the lungs for bacterial growth since these white blood cells are important in responding to bacterial infection. Host mechanisms to encourage tissue repair may inadvertently allow bacterial infection. Infection also induces the production of systemic glucocorticoids that can reduce inflammation to preserve tissue integrity but allow increased bacterial growth.

The pathophysiology of influenza is significantly influenced by which receptors influenza viruses bind to during entry into cells. Mammalian influenza viruses preferentially bind to sialic acids connected to the rest of the oligosaccharide by an α-2,6 link, most commonly found in various respiratory cells, such as respiratory and retinal epithelial cells. AIVs prefer sialic acids with an α-2,3 linkage, which are most common in birds in gastrointestinal epithelial cells and in humans in the lower respiratory tract. Furthermore, cleavage of the HA protein into HA1, the binding subunit, and HA2, the fusion subunit, is performed by different proteases, affecting which cells can be infected. For mammalian influenza viruses and low pathogenic AIVs, cleavage is extracellular, which limits infection to cells that have the appropriate proteases, whereas, for highly pathogenic AIVs, cleavage is intracellular and performed by ubiquitous proteases, which allows for infection of a greater variety of cells, thereby contributing to more severe disease.

IMMUNOLOGY

Cells possess sensors to detect viral RNA, which can then induce interferon production. Interferons mediate the expression of antiviral proteins and proteins that recruit immune cells to the infection site, and they also notify nearby uninfected cells of infection. Some infected cells release pro-inflammatory cytokines that recruit immune cells to the site of infection. Immune cells control viral infection by killing infected cells and phagocytizing viral particles and apoptotic cells. An exacerbated immune response, however, can harm the host organism through a cytokine storm. To counter the immune response, influenza viruses encode various non-structural proteins, including NS1, NEP, PB1-F2, and PA-X, that are involved in curtailing the host immune response by suppressing interferon production and host gene expression.

B cells, a type of white blood cell, produce antibodies that bind to influenza antigens HA and NA (or HEF) and other proteins to a lesser degree. Once bound to these proteins, antibodies block virions from binding to cellular receptors, neutralizing the virus. The antibody response to influenza in humans is typically robust and long-lasting, especially for ICV and IDV since HEF is antigenically stable. In other words, people exposed to a certain strain in childhood still possess antibodies to that strain at a reasonable level later in life, which can provide some protection to related strains. There is, however, an "original antigenic sin", in which the first HA subtype a person is exposed to influences the antibody-based immune response to future infections and vaccines.

ANTIVIRAL CHEMOPROPHYLAXIS

Influenza can be prevented or reduced in severity by post-exposure prophylaxis with the antiviral drugs oseltamivir, which can be taken orally by those at least three months old, and zanamivir, which can be inhaled by those above seven years of age. Chemoprophylaxis is most useful for individuals at high risk of developing complications and those who cannot receive the flu vaccine due to contraindications or lack of effectiveness. Post-exposure chemoprophylaxis is only recommended if oseltamivir is taken within 48 hours of contact with a confirmed or suspected influenza case and zanamivir within 36 hours. It is recommended that it be offered to people who have yet to receive a vaccine for the current flu season, who have been vaccinated less than two weeks since contact if there is a significant mismatch between the vaccine and circulating strains, or during an outbreak in a closed setting regardless of vaccination history.

INFECTION CONTROL

Hand hygiene is important in reducing the spread of influenza. This includes frequent handwashing with soap and water, using alcohol-based hand sanitizers, and not touching one's eyes, nose, and mouth with one's hands. Covering one's nose and mouth when coughing or sneezing is important. Other methods to limit influenza transmission include staying home when sick, avoiding contact with others until one day after symptoms end, and disinfecting surfaces likely to be contaminated by the virus, such as doorknobs. Health education through media and posters is often used to remind people of the aforementioned etiquette and hygiene.

There is uncertainty about the use of masks since research thus far has not shown a significant reduction in seasonal influenza with mask usage. Likewise, the effectiveness of screening at points of entry into countries is not well researched. Social distancing measures such as school closures, avoiding contact with infected people via isolation or quarantine, and limiting mass gatherings may reduce transmission, but these measures are often expensive, unpopular, and difficult to implement. Consequently, the commonly recommended methods of infection control are respiratory etiquette, hand hygiene, and mask-wearing, which are inexpensive and easy to perform. Pharmaceutical measures are effective but may not be available in the early stages of an outbreak.

In health care settings, infected individuals may be cohorted or assigned to individual rooms. Protective clothing such as masks, gloves, and gowns is recommended when coming into contact with infected individuals if there is a risk of exposure to infected bodily fluids. Keeping patients in negative pressure rooms and avoiding aerosol-producing activities may help, but special air handling and ventilation systems are not considered necessary to prevent the spread of influenza in the air. In residential homes, new admissions may need to be closed until the spread of influenza is controlled. When discharging patients to care homes, it is important to take care if there is a known influenza outbreak.

Since influenza viruses circulate in animals such as birds and pigs, prevention of transmission from these animals is important. Water treatment, the indoor raising of animals, quarantining sick animals, vaccination, and biosecurity are the primary measures used. Placing poultry houses and piggeries on high ground away from high-density farms, backyard farms, live poultry markets, and bodies of water help to minimize contact with wild birds. Closure of live poultry markets appears to be the most effective measure and has shown to be effective at controlling the spread of H5N1, H7N9, and H9N2. Other biosecurity measures include cleaning and disinfecting facilities and vehicles, banning visits to poultry farms, not bringing birds intended for slaughter back to farms, changing clothes, disinfecting footbaths, and treating food and water.

If live poultry markets are not closed, then "clean days" when unsold poultry is removed and facilities are disinfected and "no carry-over" policies to eliminate infectious material before new poultry arrive can be used to reduce the spread of influenza viruses. If a novel influenza virus has breached the aforementioned biosecurity measures, then rapid detection to stamp it out via quarantining, decontamination, and culling may be necessary to prevent the virus from becoming endemic. Vaccines exist for avian H5, H7, and H9 subtypes that are used in some countries. In China, for example, vaccination of domestic birds against H7N9 successfully limited its spread, indicating that vaccination may be an effective strategy if used in combination with other measures to limit transmission.

SWINE FLU

Swine influenza is an infection caused by several types of swine influenza viruses. Swine influenza virus (SIV) or swine-origin influenza virus (S-OIV) is any strain of the influenza family of viruses that is endemic in pigs. As of 2009, the known SIV strains include influenza C and the subtypes of influenza A known as H1N1, H1N2, H2N1, H3N1, H3N2, and H2N3.

Swine influenza virus is common throughout pig populations worldwide. Transmission of the virus from pigs to humans is not common and does not always lead to human flu, often resulting only in the production of antibodies in the blood. If transmission causes human flu, it is called zoonotic swine flu. People with regular exposure to pigs are at increased risk of swine flu infection.

Around the mid-20th century, identification of influenza subtypes became possible, allowing accurate diagnosis of transmission to humans. Since then, only 50 such transmissions have been confirmed. These strains of swine flu rarely pass from human to human. Symptoms of zoonotic swine flu in humans are similar to those of influenza and of influenza-like illness in general, namely chills, fever, sore throat, muscle pains, severe headache, coughing, weakness, shortness of breath, and general discomfort.

It is estimated that in the 2009 flu pandemic 11–21% of the then global population (of about 6.8 billion), or around 700 million to 1.4 billion people, contracted the illness—more in absolute terms than the Spanish flu pandemic. There were 18,449 confirmed fatalities. However, in a 2012 study, the CDC estimated more than 284,000 possible fatalities worldwide, with a range from 150,000 to 575,000. In August 2010, the World Health Organization declared the swine flu pandemic officially over.

Subsequent cases of swine flu were reported in India in 2015, with over 31,156 positive test cases and 1,841 deaths up to March 2015.

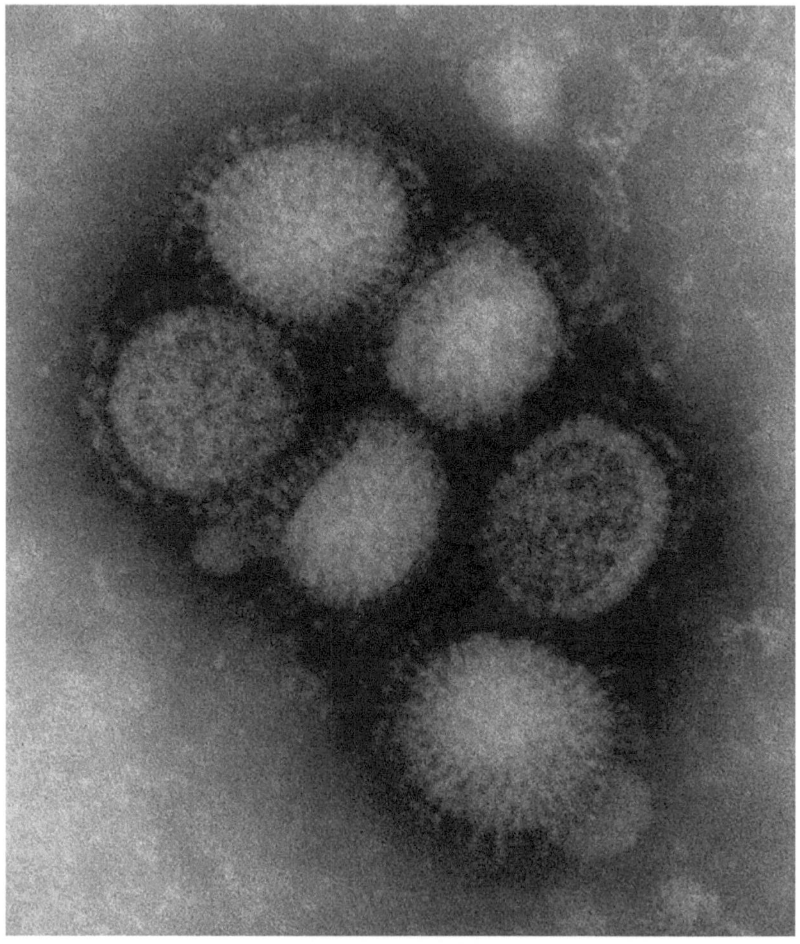

Fig. 2.5Reassorted H1N1 Influenza Virus

In pigs, a swine influenza infection produces fever, lethargy, sneezing, coughing, difficulty breathing, and decreased appetite. In some cases, the infection can cause miscarriage. Although mortality is usually low (around 1–4%), the virus can produce weight loss and poor growth, causing economic loss to farmers. Infected pigs can lose up to 12 pounds of body weight over a three- to four-week period. Swine have receptors to which both avian and mammalian influenza viruses are able to bind; this leads to the virus being able to evolve and mutate into different forms. Influenza A is responsible for infecting swine and was first identified in the summer of 1918. Pigs have often been seen as "mixing vessels", which help to change and evolve strains of disease that are then passed on to other mammals, such as humans.

Direct transmission of a swine flu virus from pigs to humans is occasionally possible (zoonotic swine flu).[citation needed] In all, 50 cases are known to have occurred since the first report in medical literature in 1958, which have resulted in a total of six deaths. Of these six people, one was pregnant, one had leukemia, one had Hodgkin's lymphoma and two were known to be previously healthy. One of these had unknown whereabouts. Despite these apparently low numbers of infections, the true rate of infection may be higher, since most cases only cause very mild disease, and will probably never be reported or diagnosed.

According to the United States Centers for Disease Control and Prevention (CDC), in humans the symptoms of the 2009 "swine flu" H1N1 virus are similar to influenza and influenza-like illness in general. Symptoms include fever, cough, sore throat, watery eyes, body aches, shortness of breath, headache, weight loss, chills, sneezing, runny nose, coughing, dizziness, abdominal pain, lack of appetite, and fatigue. The 2009 outbreak showed an increased percentage of patients reporting diarrhea and vomiting as well. The 2009 H1N1 virus is not zoonotic swine flu, as it is not transmitted from pigs to humans, but from person to person through airborne droplets.

Because these symptoms are not specific to swine flu, a differential diagnosis of probable swine flu requires not only symptoms but also a high likelihood of swine flu due to the person's recent and past medical history. For example, during the 2009 swine flu outbreak in the United States, the CDC advised physicians to "consider swine influenza infection in the differential diagnosis of patients with acute febrile respiratory illness who have either been in contact with persons with confirmed swine flu or who were in one of the five U.S. states that have reported swine flu cases or in Mexico during the seven days preceding their illness onset." A diagnosis of confirmed swine flu requires laboratory testing of a respiratory sample (a simple nose and throat swab).

The most common cause of death is respiratory failure. Other causes of death are pneumonia (leading to sepsis), high fever (leading to neurological problems), dehydration (from excessive vomiting and diarrhea), electrolyte imbalance, and kidney failure. Fatalities are more likely in young children and the elderly.

Swine influenza was first proposed to be a disease related to human flu during the 1918 flu pandemic when pigs became ill at the same time as humans. The first identification of an influenza virus as a cause of disease in pigs occurred about ten years later, in 1930. For the following 60 years, swine influenza strains were almost exclusively H1N1. Then, between 1997 and 2002, new strains of three different subtypes and five different genotypes emerged as causes of influenza among pigs in North America. In 1997–1998, H3N2 strains emerged. These strains, which include genes derived by reassortment from human, swine, and avian viruses, have become a major cause of swine influenza in North America. Reassortment between H1N1 and H3N2 produced H1N2. In 1999 in Canada, a strain of H4N6 crossed the species barrier from birds to pigs but was contained on a single farm.

The H1N1 form of swine flu is one of the descendants of the strain that caused the 1918 flu pandemic. As well as persisting in pigs, the descendants of the 1918 virus have also circulated in humans through the 20th century, contributing to the normal seasonal epidemics of influenza. However, direct transmission from pigs to humans is rare, with only 12 recorded cases in the U.S. since 2005. Nevertheless, the retention of influenza strains in pigs after these strains have disappeared from the human population might make pigs a reservoir where influenza viruses could persist, later emerging to reinfect humans once human immunity to these strains has waned.

Swine flu has been reported numerous times as a zoonosis in humans, usually with limited distribution, rarely with a widespread distribution. Outbreaks in swine are common and cause significant economic losses in the industry, primarily by causing stunting and extended time to market. For example, this disease costs the British meat industry about £65 million every year.

The 1918 flu pandemic in humans was associated with H1N1 and influenza appearing in pigs; this may reflect a zoonosis either from swine to humans, or from humans to swine. Although it is not certain in which direction the virus was transferred, some evidence suggests, in this case, pigs caught the disease from humans. For instance, swine influenza was only noted as a new disease of pigs in 1918, after the first large outbreaks of influenza amongst people. Although a recent phylogenetic analysis of more recent strains of influenza in humans, birds, animals, and many others, including swine, suggests the 1918 outbreak in humans followed a reassortment event within a mammal, the exact origin of the 1918 strain remains elusive. It is estimated that anywhere from 50 to 100 million people were killed worldwide.

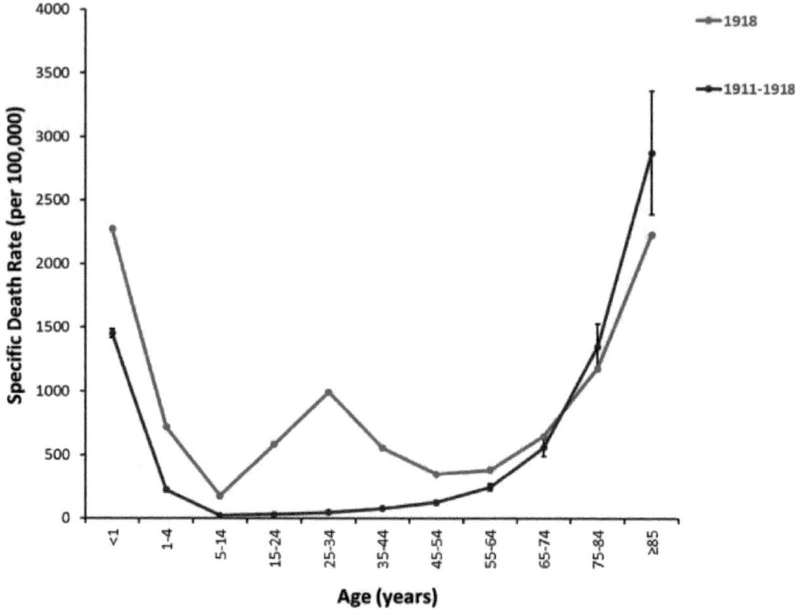

Fig. 2.6 Mortality rate of Influenza

CHAPTER THREE

THE HIV/AIDS PANDEMIC (GLOBAL EPIDEMIC)

Acquired immunodeficiency syndrome (AIDS) is a chronic, potentially life-threatening condition caused by the human immunodeficiency virus (HIV). By damaging your immune system, HIV interferes with your body's ability to fight infection and disease. HIV is a sexually transmitted infection (STI). It can also be spread by contact with infected blood or from mother to child during pregnancy, childbirth, or breastfeeding. Without medication, it may take years before HIV weakens your immune system to the point that you have AIDS. There's no cure for HIV/AIDS, but medications can dramatically slow the progression of the disease. These drugs have reduced AIDS deaths in many developed nations.

Human Immunodeficiency Virus, is considered by some people a global pandemic. However, the WHO currently uses the term 'global epidemic' to describe HIV. As of 2018, approximately 37.9 million people are infected with HIV globally. There were about 770,000 deaths from AIDS in 2018. The 2015 Global Burden of Disease Study, in a report published in The Lancet, estimated that the global incidence of HIV infection peaked in 1997 at 3.3 million per year. Global incidence fell rapidly from 1997 to 2005, to about

2.6 million per year, but remained stable from 2005 to 2015.

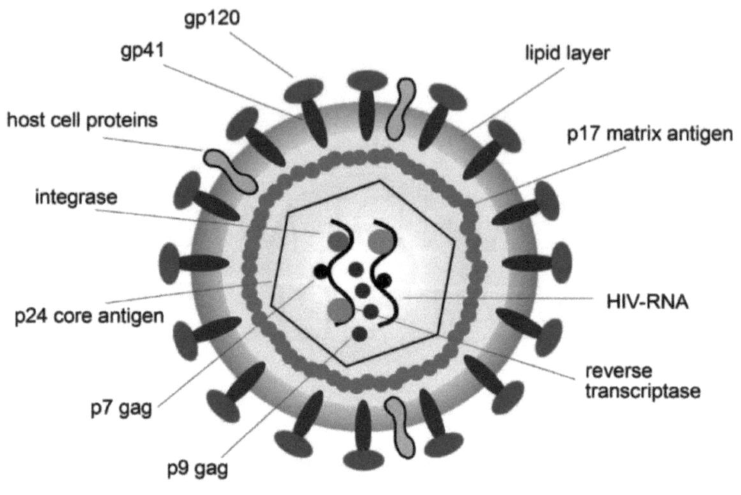

Fig. 3.1 Structure of HIV Virus

Sub-Saharan Africa is the region most affected. In 2018, an estimated 61% of new HIV infections occurred in this region. Prevalence ratios are "In western and central Europe and North America, the low and declining incidence of HIV and mortality among people infected with HIV over the last 17 years has seen the incidence: prevalence ratio fall from 0.06 in 2000 to 0.03 in 2017. Strong and steady reductions in new HIV infections and mortality among people infected with HIV in eastern and southern Africa have pushed the ratio down from 0.11 in 2000 to 0.04 in 2017. Progress has been more gradual in Asia and the Pacific (0.05 in 2017), Latin America (0.06 in 2017), the Caribbean (0.05 in 2017), and western and central Africa (0.06 in 2017). The incidence: prevalence ratios of the Middle East and North Africa (0.08 in 2017) and eastern Europe and central Asia (0.09 in 2017)". South Africa has the largest population of people with HIV in any country in the world, at 7.06 million as of 2017. In Tanzania, HIV/AIDS was reported to have a prevalence of 4.5% among Tanzanian adults aged 15–49 in 2017.

South & South-East Asia (a region with about 2 billion people as of 2010, over 30% of the global population) has an estimated 4 million cases (12% of all people infected with HIV), with about 250,000 deaths in 2010. Approximately 2.5 million of these cases are in India, where however the prevalence is only about 0.3% (somewhat higher than that found in Western and Central Europe or Canada). Prevalence is lowest in East Asia at 0.1%.

In 2019, approximately 1.2 million people in the United States had HIV; 13% did not realize that they were infected.

In 2020, 106,890 people were living with HIV in the UK and 614 died (99 of these from Covid-19 comorbidity).

In Australia, as of 2020, there were about 29,090 cases. In Canada as of 2016, there were about 63,110 cases. Reconstruction of its genetic history shows that the HIV pandemic almost certainly originated in Kinshasa, the capital of the Democratic Republic of the Congo, around 1920. AIDS was first recognized in 1981, in 1983 HIV was discovered and identified as the cause of AIDS, and by 2009 AIDS had caused nearly 30 million deaths.

Since the first case of HIV/AIDS was reported in 1981, this virus, although rare, continues to be one of the most prevalent and deadliest pandemics worldwide. The Center for Disease Control mentions that HIV disease continues to be a serious health issue for several parts of the world. Worldwide, there were about 1.7 million new cases of HIV reported in 2018. About 37.9 million people were living with HIV around the world in 2018, and 24.5 million of them were receiving medicines to treat HIV, called antiretroviral therapy (ART). In addition, roughly an estimated 770,000 people have died from AIDS-related illnesses in 2018.

Globally, individuals suffer from HIV/AIDS; yet, there has also been a common trend as far as prevalence in cases and regions most affected by the disease. The CDC reports that areas like the Sub-Saharan Africa region are the most affected by HIV and AIDS worldwide, and account for approximately 61% of all new HIV infections. Other regions significantly affected by HIV and AIDS include Asia and the Pacific, Latin America and the Caribbean, Eastern Europe, and Central Asia.

Worldwide a common stigma and discrimination are surrounding HIV/AIDS. Respectively, infected patients are more subject to judgment, harassment, and acts of violence and come from marginalized areas where it is common to engage in illegal practices in exchange for money, drugs, or other exchangeable forms of currency.

AVERT, an international HIV and AIDS charity created in 1986, makes continuous efforts to prioritize, normalize, and provide the latest information and education programs on HIV and AIDS for individuals and areas most affected by this disease worldwide. AVERT suggested that, discrimination and other human rights violations may occur in health care settings, barring people from accessing health services or enjoying quality health care.

Accessibility to tests has also played a significant role in the response and speed to which nations take action. Approximately 81% of people with HIV globally knew their HIV status in 2019. The remaining 19% (about 7.1 million people) still need access to HIV testing services. HIV testing is an essential gateway to HIV prevention, treatment, care, and support services. It is crucial to have HIV tests available for individuals worldwide since it can help individuals detect the status of their disease from an early onset, seek help, and prevent further spread through the practice of suggestive safety precautions.

There were approximately 38 million people across the globe with HIV/AIDS in 2019. Of these, 36.2 million were adults and 1.8 million were children under 15 years old.

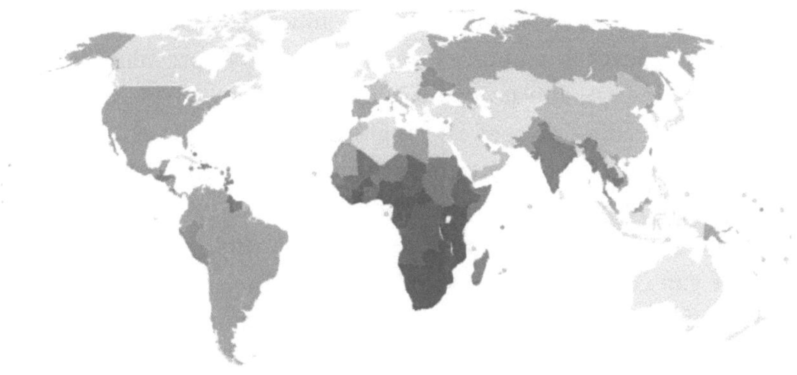

Fig. 3.2 Disability-adjusted life year for HIV & AIDS per 100,000 inhabitants

BY REGION

SUB-SAHARAN AFRICA

Sub-Saharan Africa remains the hardest-hit region. HIV infection is becoming endemic in sub-Saharan Africa, which is home to just over 12% of the world's population but two-thirds of all people infected with HIV. The adult HIV prevalence rate is 5.0% and between 21.6 million and 24.1 million total are affected. However, the actual prevalence varies between regions. Presently, Southern Africa is the hardest-hit region, with adult prevalence rates exceeding 20% in most countries in the region, and 30% in Eswatini and Botswana. Analysis of prevalence across sub-Saharan Africa between 2000 and 2017 found high variation in prevalence at a subnational level, with some countries demonstrating a more than the five-fold difference in prevalence between different districts.

Eastern Africa also experiences relatively high levels of prevalence with estimates above 10% in some countries, although there are signs that the pandemic is declining in this region. West Africa on the other hand has been much less affected by the pandemic. Several countries reportedly have prevalence rates around 2% to 3%, and no country has rates above 10%. In Nigeria and Côte d'Ivoire, two of the region's most populous countries, between 5 and 7% of adults are reported to carry the virus.

Across Sub-Saharan Africa, more women are infected with HIV than men, with 13 women infected for every 10 infected men. This gender gap continues to grow. Throughout the region, women are being infected with HIV at earlier ages than men. The differences in infection levels between women and men are most pronounced among young people (aged 15–24 years). In this age group, there are 36 women infected with HIV for every 10 men. The widespread prevalence of sexually transmitted diseases, the promiscuous culture, the practice of scarification, unsafe blood transfusions, and the poor state of hygiene and nutrition in some areas may all be facilitating factors in the transmission of HIV-1 (Bentwich et al., 1995).

Mother-to-child transmission is another contributing factor in the transmission of HIV-1 in developing nations. Due to a lack of testing, a shortage in antenatal therapies, and through the feeding of contaminated breast milk, 590,000 infants born in developing countries are infected with HIV-1 per year. In 2000, the World Health Organization estimated that 25% of the units of blood transfused in Africa were not tested for HIV and that 10% of HIV infections in Africa were transmitted via blood.

Poor economic conditions (leading to the use of dirty needles in healthcare clinics) and lack of education contribute to high rates of infection. In some African countries, 25% or more of the working adult population is HIV-positive.

AIDS-denialist policies have impeded the creation of effective programs for the distribution of antiretroviral drugs. Denialist policies by former South African President Thabo Mbeki's administration led to several hundred thousand unnecessary deaths. UNAIDS estimates that in 2005 there were 5.5 million people in South Africa infected with HIV — 12.4% of the population. This was an increase of 200,000 people since 2003.

Although HIV infection rates are much lower in Nigeria than in other African countries, the size of Nigeria's population meant that by the end of 2003, there were an estimated 3.6 million people infected. On the other hand, Uganda, Zambia, Senegal, and most recently Botswana have begun intervention and educational measures to slow the spread of HIV, and Uganda has succeeded in actually reducing its HIV infection rate.

MIDDLE EAST AND NORTH AFRICA

HIV/AIDS prevalence among the adult population (15-49) in the Middle East and North Africa is estimated at less than 0.1 between 1990 and 2018. This is the lowest prevalence rate compared to other regions in the world.

In the MENA, roughly 240,000 people are living with HIV as of 2018 and Iran accounted for approximately one-quarter (61,000) of the population with HIV followed by Sudan (59,000). As well, Sudan (5,200), Iran (4,400), and Egypt (3,600) took up more than 60% of the number of new infections in the MENA (20,000). Roughly two-thirds of AIDS-related deaths in this region happened in these countries for the year 2018.

Although the prevalence is low, concerns remain in this region. First, unlike the global downward trend in new HIV infections and AIDS-related deaths, the numbers have continuously increased in the MENA. Second, compared to the global rate of antiretroviral therapy (62%), the MENA region's rate is far below (32%). The low participation of ART increases not only the number of AIDS-related deaths but the risk of mother-to-baby HIV infections, in which the MENA (24.7%) shows relatively high rates compared to other regions, for example, southern Africa (10%), Asia, and the Pacific (17%).

CHRONOLOGY

The 1980s

In 1981, cases of a rare lung infection called Pneumocystis carinii pneumonia (PCP) were found in five young, previously healthy men in Los Angeles. At the same time, there were reports of a group of men in New York and California with an unusually aggressive cancer named Kaposi's Sarcoma.

In December 1981, the first cases of PCP were reported in people who inject drugs.

By the end of the year, there were 270 reported cases of severe immune deficiency among men - 121 of them had died.

In June 1982, a group of cases among gay men in Southern California suggested that the cause of the immune deficiency was sexual and the syndrome was initially called gay-related immune deficiency (or GRID).

Later that month, the disease was reported in hemophiliacs and Haitians leading many to believe it had originated in Haiti.

In September, the CDC used the term 'AIDS' (acquired immune deficiency syndrome) for the first time, describing it as " a disease at least moderately predictive of a defect in cell-mediated immunity, occurring in a person with no known cause for diminished resistance to that disease."

AIDS cases were also being reported in several European countries.

In Uganda, doctors reported cases of a new, fatal wasting disease locally known as 'slim'.

By this point, several AIDS-specific organizations had been set up including the San Francisco AIDS Foundation (SFAF) in the USA and the Terrence Higgins Trust in the UK.

In January 1983, AIDS was reported among the female partners of men who had the disease suggesting it could be passed on via heterosexual sexual contact.

In May, doctors at the Pasteur Institute in France reported the discovery of a new retrovirus called lymphadenopathy-associated Virus (or LAV) that could be the cause of AIDS.

In June, the first reports of AIDS in children hinted that it could be passed via casual contact but this was later ruled out and it was concluded that they had probably directly acquired AIDS from their mothers before, during, or shortly after birth.

By September, the CDC identified all major routes of transmission and ruled out transmission by casual contact, food, water, air, or surfaces.

The CDC also published their first set of recommended precautions for healthcare workers and allied health professionals to prevent "AIDS transmission".

In November, the World Health Organization (WHO) held its first meeting to assess the global AIDS situation and began international surveillance.

By the end of the year, the number of AIDS cases in the USA had risen to 3,064 - of this number, 1,292 had died.

In April 1984, the National Cancer Institute announced they had found the cause of AIDS, the retrovirus HTLV-III. In a joint conference with the Pasteur Institute, they announced that LAV and HTLV-III are identical and the likely cause of AIDS. A blood test was created to screen for the virus with the hope that a vaccine would be developed in two years.

In July, the CDC stated that avoiding injecting drug use and sharing needles "should also be effective in preventing transmission of the virus."

In October, bathhouses in San Francisco were closed due to high-risk sexual activity. New York and Los Angeles followed suit within a year.

By the end of 1984, there had been 7,699 AIDS cases and 3,665 AIDS deaths in the USA with 762 cases reported in Europe.

In Amsterdam, Netherlands, the first needle and syringe program was set up with growing concerns about HTLV-III/LAV.

In March 1985, the U.S Food and Drug Administration (FDA) licensed the first commercial blood test, ELISA, to detect antibodies to the virus. Blood banks began to screen the USA blood supply.

In April, the U.S. Department of Health and Human Services (HHS) and the World Health Organization (WHO) hosted the first International AIDS Conference in Atlanta Georgia.

Ryan White, a teenager from Indiana, USA who acquired AIDS through contaminated blood products used to treat his hemophilia was banned from school.

On 2 October, the actor Rock Hudson dies from AIDS - the first high-profile fatality. He left $250,000 to set up the American Foundation for AIDS Research (amfAR).

In December, the U.S. Public Health Service issued the first recommendations for preventing mother to child transmission of the virus.

By the end of 1985, every region in the world had reported at least one case of AIDS, with 20,303 cases in total.

In May 1986, the International Committee on the Taxonomy of Viruses said that the virus that causes AIDS will officially be called HIV (human immunodeficiency virus) instead of HTLV-III/LAV.

By the end of the year, 85 countries had reported 38,401 cases of AIDS to the World Health Organization. By region these were; Africa 2,323, Americas 31,741, Asia 84, Europe 3,858, and Oceania 395.

In February 1987, the WHO launched The Global Program on AIDS to raise awareness; generate evidence-based policies; provide technical and financial support to countries; conduct research; promote participation by NGOs, and promote the rights of people living with HIV.

In March, the FDA approved the first antiretroviral drug, zidovudine (AZT), as a treatment for HIV. In April, the FDA approved the western blot blood test kit, a more specific HIV antibody test. In July, the WHO confirmed that HIV could be passed from mother to child during breastfeeding. In October, AIDS became the first illness debated in the United Nations (UN) General

Assembly.

By December, 71,751 cases of AIDS had been reported to the WHO, with 47,022 of these in the USA. The WHO estimated that 5-10 million people were living with HIV worldwide.

In 1988, the WHO declared 1st December as the first World AIDS Day.

The groundwork was laid for a nationwide HIV and AIDS care system in the USA that was later funded by the Ryan White CARE Act.

In March 1989, 145 countries had reported 142,000 AIDS cases. However, the WHO estimated there were up to 400,000 cases worldwide.

In June, the CDC released the first guidelines to prevent PCP - an opportunistic infection that was a major cause of death among people with AIDS.

The number of reported AIDS cases in the USA reached 100,000.

The 1990s

On 8 April 1990, Ryan White died of an AIDS-related illness aged 18. In June, the 6th International AIDS Conference in San Francisco protested against the USA's immigration policy which stopped people with HIV from entering the country. NGOs boycotted the conference. In July, the USA enacted the Americans with Disabilities Act (ADA) which prohibits discrimination against those with disabilities including people living with HIV. In October, the FDA approved the use of zidovudine (AZT) to treat children with AIDS. By the end of 1990, over 307,000 AIDS cases had been officially reported with the actual number estimated to be closer to a million. Between 8-10 million people were thought to be living with HIV worldwide.

In 1991, the Visual AIDS Artists Caucus launched the Red Ribbon Project to create a symbol of compassion for people living with HIV and their carers. The red ribbon became an international symbol of AIDS awareness. On 7 November, professional basketball player Earvin (Magic) Johnson announced he had HIV and retired from the sport, planning to educate young people about the virus. This announcement helped begin to dispel the stereotype, still widely held in the US and elsewhere, of HIV as a 'gay' disease.

The 1992 International AIDS Conference scheduled to be held in Boston, USA was moved to Amsterdam due to USA immigration rules on people living with HIV. Tennis star Arthur Ashe revealed he became infected with HIV as the result of a blood transfusion in 1983. In May, the FDA licensed a 10-minute testing kit that could be used by healthcare professionals to detect HIV-1.

In March 1993, the USA Congress voted overwhelmingly to retain the ban on entry into the country for people living with HIV. The CDC added pulmonary tuberculosis, recurrent pneumonia, and invasive cervical cancer to the list of AIDS indicators. Over 700,000 people were thought to have the virus in Asia and the Pacific. By the end of 1993, there were an estimated 2.5 million AIDS cases globally.

In August 1994, the USA Public Health Service recommended the use of AZT to prevent the mother-to-child transmission of HIV. In December, the FDA approved an oral HIV test - the first non-blood HIV test.

In June 1995, the FDA approved the first protease inhibitor beginning a new era of highly active antiretroviral treatment (HAART). Once incorporated into clinical practice HAART brought about an immediate decline of between 60% and 80% in rates of AIDS-related deaths and hospitalization in those countries which could afford it. By the end of the year, there were an estimated 4.7 million new HIV infections - 2.5 million in southeast Asia and 1.9 million in sub-Saharan Africa.

In 1996, the Joint United Nations Programme on AIDS (UNAIDS) was established to advocate for global action on the epidemic and coordinate the response to HIV and AIDS across the UN. The 11th International AIDS Conference in Vancouver highlighted the effectiveness of HAART leading to a period of optimism. The FDA approved the first home testing kit; a viral load test to measure the level of HIV in the blood; the first non-nucleoside transcriptase inhibitor (NNRTI) drug (nevirapine); and the first HIV urine test. New HIV outbreaks were detected in Eastern Europe, the former Soviet Union, India, Vietnam, Cambodia, and China among others. By the end of 1996, the estimated number of people living with HIV was 23 million.

In September 1997, the FDA approved Combivir, a combination of two antiretroviral drugs, taken as a single daily tablet, making it easier for people living with HIV to take their medication. UNAIDS estimated that 30 million people had HIV worldwide equating to 16,000 new infections a day.

In 1999, the WHO announced that AIDS was the fourth biggest cause of death worldwide and the number one killer in Africa. An estimated 33 million people were living with HIV and 14 million people had died from AIDS since the start of the epidemic.

The 2000s

In July, UNAIDS negotiated with five pharmaceutical companies to reduce antiretroviral drug prices for developing countries. In September, the United Nations adopted the Millennium Development Goals which included a specific goal to reverse the spread of HIV, malaria, and TB.

In June 2001, the United Nations (UN) General Assembly called for the creation of a "global fund" to support efforts by countries and organizations to combat the spread of HIV through prevention, treatment, and care including buying medication. After generic drug manufacturers, such as Cipla in India, began producing discounted, generic forms of HIV medicines for developing countries, several major pharmaceutical manufacturers agreed to further reduce drug prices. In November, the World Trade Organization (WTO) announced the Doha Declaration which allowed developing countries to manufacture generic medications to combat public health crises like HIV.

In April 2002, the Global Fund approved its first round of grants totaling $600 million. In July, UNAIDS reported that AIDS was now by far the leading cause of death in sub-Saharan Africa. Also in July, South Africa's Constitutional Court orders the government to make the HIV drug nevirapine available to all HIV-positive pregnant women and their newborn children following a legal challenge by the Treatment Action Campaign. In November, the FDA approved the first rapid HIV test with 99.6% accuracy and a result in 20 minutes.

In January 2003, President George W. Bush announced the creation of the United States President's Emergency Plan For AIDS Relief (PEPFAR), a $15 billion, five-year plan to combat AIDS, primarily in countries with a high number of HIV infections. In December, the WHO announced the "3 by 5" initiative to bring HIV treatment to 3 million people by 2005.

In 2006, male circumcision was found to reduce the risk of female-to-male HIV transmission by 60%.81 Since then, the WHO and UNAIDS have emphasized that male circumcision should be considered in areas with high HIV and low male circumcision prevalence.

In May 2007, the WHO and UNAIDS issued new guidance recommending "provider-initiated" HIV testing in healthcare settings. This aimed to widen knowledge of HIV status and greatly increase access to HIV treatment and prevention.

The 2010s

In January 2010, the travel ban preventing HIV-positive people from entering the USA was lifted. In July, the CAPRISA 004 microbicide trial was hailed a success after results showed that the microbicide gel reduces the risk of HIV infection in women by 40%. Results from the iPrEx trial showed a reduction in HIV acquisition of 44% among men who took pre-exposure prophylaxis (PrEP).

In 2011, results from the HPTN 052 trial showed that early initiation of antiretroviral treatment reduced the risk of HIV transmission by 96% among serodiscordant couples. In August, the FDA approved Complera, the second all-in-one fixed-dose combination tablet, expanding the treatment options available for people living with HIV.

In July 2012, the FDA approved PrEP for HIV-negative people to prevent the sexual transmission of HIV. For the first time, the majority of people eligible for treatment were receiving it (54%).

In 2013, UNAIDS reported that AIDS-related deaths had fallen 30% since their peak in 2005. An estimated 35 million people were living with HIV. In September 2014, new UNAIDS "Fast Track" targets called for the dramatic scaling-up of HIV prevention and treatment programs to avert 28 million new infections and end the epidemic as a public health issue by 2030. UNAIDS also launched the ambitious 90-90-90 targets which aim for 90% of people living with HIV to be diagnosed, 90% of those diagnosed to be accessing antiretroviral treatment, and 90% of those accessing treatment to achieve viral suppression by 2020.

In July 2015, UNAIDS announced that the Millennium Development Goal (MDG) relating to HIV and AIDS had been reached six months ahead of schedule. The target of MDG 6 – halting and reversing the spread of HIV – saw 15 million people receive treatment. In September, the WHO launched new treatment guidelines recommending that all people living with HIV should receive antiretroviral treatment, regardless of their CD4 count, and as soon as possible after their diagnosis.

In October, UNAIDS released their 2016-2021 strategy in line with the new Sustainable Development Goals (SDGs), which called for an acceleration in the global HIV response to reach critical HIV prevention and treatment targets and achieve zero discrimination. The number of people in Russia living with HIV reached one million. Newly released figures also showed 64% of all new HIV diagnoses in Europe occurred in Russia. UNAIDS announced that 18.2 million people were on ART, including 910 000 children, double the number five years earlier. However, achieving increased ART access means a greater risk of drug resistance, and the WHO released a report on dealing with this growing issue. AVERT marked its 30th anniversary - having provided HIV and AIDS information from the start of the epidemic we continue our work to empower people through knowledge to avert HIV.

For the first time, more than half of the global population living with HIV are receiving antiretroviral treatment, a record of 19.5 million people. Organizations around the world endorse "Undetectable = Untransmittable"(U=U). This anti-stigma slogan launched by the Prevention Access Campaign is based on robust scientific evidence that people who have adhered to treatment and achieved an undetectable viral load cannot pass the virus on. In 2017 'U=U' becomes a defining message of the HIV response in many well-resourced countries, but fails to have the same impact in lower resource settings, where viral-load monitoring is more difficult.

New infections have fallen by a third in East and Southern Africa over the last six years, with particular decreases among young women and girls. It is thought that this is partly due to the success of the DREAMS initiative, which aimed to reduce HIV infections among women and girls in sub-Saharan Africa by providing them with economic opportunities as well as better HIV services and education.

SYMPTOMS

The symptoms of HIV and AIDS vary, depending on the phase of infection.

PRIMARY INFECTION (ACUTE HIV)

Some people infected by HIV develop a flu-like illness within two to four weeks after the virus enters the body. This illness, known as primary (acute) HIV infection, may last for a few weeks. Possible signs and symptoms include:

Fever, Headache, Muscle aches and joint pain, Rash, Sore throat and painful mouth sores, Swollen lymph glands, mainly on the neck, Diarrhea, Weight loss, Cough, Night sweats.

These symptoms can be so mild that you might not even notice them. However, the amount of virus in your bloodstream (viral load) is quite high at this time. As a result, the infection spreads more easily during primary infection than during the next stage.

CLINICAL LATENT INFECTION (CHRONIC HIV)

In this stage of infection, HIV is still present in the body and white blood cells. However, many people may not have any symptoms or infections during this time.

This stage can last for many years if you're not receiving antiretroviral therapy (ART). Some people develop more severe diseases much sooner.

SYMPTOMATIC HIV INFECTION

As the virus continues to multiply and destroy your immune cells — the cells in your body that help fight off germs — you may develop mild infections or chronic signs and symptoms such as:

Fever, Fatigue, Swollen lymph nodes — often one of the first signs of HIV infection, Diarrhea, Weight loss, Oral yeast infection (thrush), Shingles (herpes zoster), Pneumonia.

PROGRESSION TO AIDS

Thanks to better antiviral treatments, most people with HIV in the U.S. today don't develop AIDS. Untreated, HIV typically turns into AIDS in about 8 to 10 years.

When AIDS occurs, your immune system has been severely damaged. You'll be more likely to develop opportunistic infections or opportunistic cancers — diseases that wouldn't usually cause illness in a person with a healthy immune system.

The signs and symptoms of some of these infections may include:

Sweats, Chills, Recurring fever, Chronic diarrhea, Swollen lymph glands, Persistent white spots or unusual lesions on your tongue or in your mouth, Persistent, unexplained fatigue, Weakness, Weight loss, Skin rashes or bumps.

CAUSES

HIV is caused by a virus. It can spread through sexual contact or blood, or from mother to child during pregnancy, childbirth, or breastfeeding.

HOW DOES HIV BECOME AIDS

HIV destroys CD4 T cells — white blood cells that play a large role in helping your body fight disease. The fewer CD4 T cells you have, the weaker your immune system becomes.

You can have an HIV infection, with few or no symptoms, for years before it turns into AIDS. AIDS is diagnosed when the CD4 T cell count falls below 200 or you have an AIDS-defining complication, such as serious infection or cancer.

HIV can spread in several ways:

By sharing needles. Sharing contaminated IV drug paraphernalia (needles and syringes) puts you at high risk of HIV and other infectious diseases, such as hepatitis.

From blood transfusions. In some cases, the virus may be transmitted through blood transfusions. American hospitals and blood banks now screen the blood supply for HIV antibodies, so this risk is very small.

During pregnancy or delivery or through breastfeeding. Infected mothers can pass the virus on to their babies. Mothers who are HIV-positive and get treatment for the infection during pregnancy can significantly lower the risk to their babies.

INFECTIONS COMMON TO HIV/AIDS

Pneumocystis pneumonia (PCP). This fungal infection can cause severe illness. Although it's declined significantly with current treatments for HIV/AIDS, in the U.S. PCP is still the most common cause of pneumonia in people infected with HIV.

Candidiasis (thrush). Candidiasis is a common HIV-related infection. It causes inflammation and a thick, white coating on your mouth, tongue, esophagus.

Tuberculosis (TB). In resource-limited nations, TB is the most common opportunistic infection associated with HIV. It's a leading cause of death among people with AIDS.

Cytomegalovirus. This common herpes virus is transmitted in body fluids such as saliva, blood, urine, semen, and breast milk. A healthy immune system inactivates the virus, and it remains dormant in your body. If your immune system weakens, the virus resurfaces — causing damage to your eyes, digestive tract, lungs, or other organs.

Cryptococcal meningitis. Meningitis is an inflammation of the membranes and fluid surrounding your brain and spinal cord (meninges). Cryptococcal meningitis is a common central nervous system infection associated with HIV, caused by a fungus found in soil.

Toxoplasmosis. This potentially deadly infection is caused by Toxoplasma gondii, a parasite spread primarily by cats. Infected cats pass the parasites in their stools, which may then spread to other animals and humans. Toxoplasmosis can cause heart disease, and seizures occur when it spreads to the brain.

CANCERS COMMON TO HIV/AIDS

Lymphoma. This cancer starts in the white blood cells. The most common early sign is painless swelling of the lymph nodes in your neck, armpit, or groin.

Kaposi's sarcoma. A tumor of the blood vessel walls, Kaposi's sarcoma usually appears as pink, red, or purple lesions on the skin and mouth. In people with darker skin, the lesions may look dark brown or black. Kaposi's sarcoma can also affect the internal organs, including the digestive tract and lungs.

OTHER COMPLICATIONS

Wasting syndrome. Untreated HIV/AIDS can cause significant weight loss, often accompanied by diarrhea, chronic weakness, and fever.

Neurological complications. HIV can cause neurological symptoms such as confusion, forgetfulness, depression, anxiety, and difficulty walking. HIV-associated neurocognitive disorders (HAND) can range from mild symptoms of behavioral changes and reduced mental functioning to severe dementia causing weakness and inability to function.

Kidney disease. HIV-associated nephropathy (HIVAN) is an inflammation of the tiny filters in your kidneys that remove excess fluid and wastes from your blood and pass them to your urine. It most often affects blacks or Hispanic people.

Liver disease. Liver disease is also a major complication, especially in people who also have hepatitis B or hepatitis C.

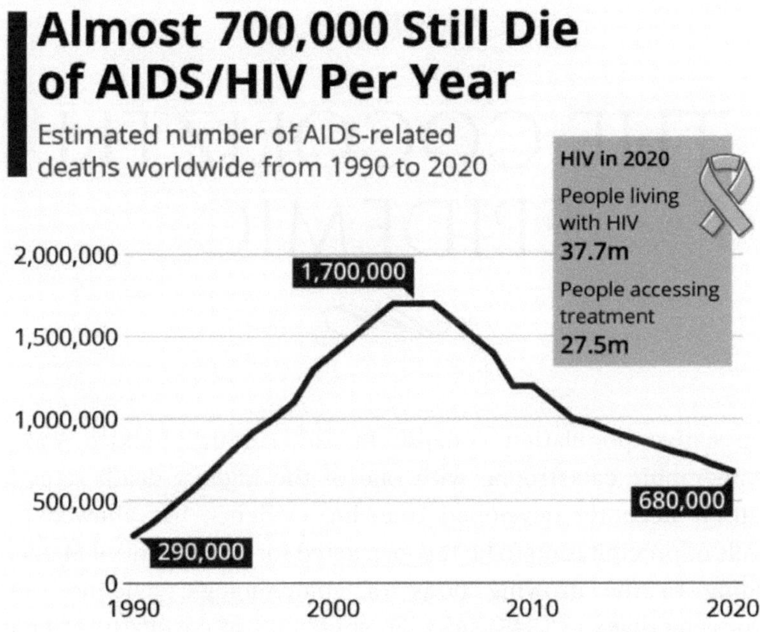

Fig. 3.3 HIV/AIDS Deaths Continue to Decline

CHAPTER FOUR

THE COCOLIZTLI EPIDEMIC

The native population collapse in 16th century Mexico was a demographic catastrophe with one of the highest death rates in history. Recently developed tree-ring evidence has allowed the levels of precipitation to be reconstructed for north-central Mexico, adding to the growing body of epidemiologic evidence and indicating that the 1545 and 1576 epidemics of cocoliztli (Nahuatl for "pest") were indigenous hemorrhagic fevers transmitted by rodent hosts and aggravated by extreme drought conditions.

The native people of Mexico experienced an epidemic disease in the wake of European conquest, beginning with the smallpox epidemic of 1519 to 1520 when 5 million to 8 million people perished. The catastrophic epidemics that began in 1545 and 1576 subsequently killed an additional 7 million to 17 million people in the highlands of Mexico. Recent epidemiologic research suggests that the events in 1545 and 1576, associated with a high death rate and referred to as cocoliztli (Nahuatl for "pest"), may have been due to indigenous hemorrhagic fevers. Tree-ring evidence, allowing reconstructions of the levels of precipitation, indicates that the worst drought to afflict North America in the past 500 years also occurred in the mid-16th century when severe drought extended at times from Mexico to the boreal forest and from the Pacific to Atlantic coasts. These droughts appear to have interacted with ecologic and sociologic conditions, magnifying the human impact of infectious disease in 16th-century Mexico.

From 1545 to 1550, Aztecs in what is today southern Mexico experienced a deadly outbreak. Anywhere from five to 15 million people died. Locally, it was known as cocoliztli, but the exact cause or causes has been a mystery for the past 500 years.

Now, a new study published in the journal Nature Ecology and Evolution suggests the outbreak could have been caused by a deadly form of salmonella.

The epidemic of cocoliztli from1545 to 1548 killed an estimated 5 million to 15 million people or up to 80% of the native population of Mexico. In absolute and relative terms the 1545 epidemic was one of the worst demographic catastrophes in human history, approaching even the Black Death of bubonic plague, which killed approximately 25 million in western Europe from 1347 to 1351 or about 50% of the regional population.

The cocoliztli epidemic from 1576 to 1578 cocoliztli epidemic killed an additional 2 to 2.5 million people or about 50% of the remaining native population. Newly introduced European and African diseases such as smallpox, measles, and typhus have long been the suspected cause of the population collapse in both 1545 and 1576 because both epidemics preferentially killed native people. But careful reanalysis of the 1545 and 1576 epidemics now indicates that they were probably hemorrhagic fevers, likely caused by an indigenous virus and carried by a rodent host. These infections appear to have been aggravated by the extreme climatic conditions of the time and by the poor living conditions and harsh treatment of the native people under the encomienda system of New Spain. The Mexican natives in the encomienda system were treated as virtual slaves, were poorly fed and clothed, and were greatly overworked as farm and mine laborers. This harsh treatment appears to have left them particularly vulnerable to epidemic disease.

Cocoliztli was a swift and highly lethal disease. Francisco Hernandez, the Proto-Medico of New Spain, former personal physician of King Phillip II and one of the most qualified physicians of the day, witnessed the symptoms of the 1576 cocoliztli infections. Hernandez described the gruesome cocoliztli symptoms with clinical accuracy. The symptoms included high fever, severe headache, vertigo, black tongue, dark urine, dysentery, severe abdominal, and thoracic pain, large nodules behind the ears that often invaded the neck and face, acute neurologic disorders, and profuse bleeding from the nose, eyes, and mouth with death frequently occurring in 3 to 4 days. These symptoms are not consistent with known European or African diseases present in Mexico during the 16th century.

The geography of the 16th century cocoliztli epidemics supports the notion that they may have been indigenous fevers carried by rodents or other hosts native to the highlands of Mexico. In 1545 the epidemic affected the northern and central high valleys of Mexico and ended in Chiapas and Guatemala. In both the 1545 and 1576 epidemics, the infections were largely absent from the warm, low-lying coastal plains on the Gulf of Mexico and Pacific coasts. This geography of disease is not consistent with the introduction of an Old World virus to Mexico, which should have affected both coastal and highland populations.

Tree-ring evidence, reconstructed rainfall over Durango, Mexico during the 16th century, adds support to the hypothesis that unusual climatic conditions may have interacted with host-population dynamics and the cocoliztli virus to aggravate the epidemics of 1545 and 1576. The tree-ring data indicate that both epidemics occurred during the 16th-century megadrought, the most severe and sustained drought to impact north-central Mexico in the past 600 years. The scenario for the climatic, ecologic, and sociologic mediation of the 16th-century cocoliztli epidemics is reminiscent of the rodent population dynamics involved in the outbreak of hantavirus pulmonary syndrome caused by the Sin Nombre Virus on the Colorado Plateau in 1993. Cocoliztli was not pulmonary and may not have been a hantavirus but may have been spread by a rodent host. If true, then the prolonged drought before the

16th-century epidemics would have reduced the available water and food resources. The animal hosts would then tend to concentrate around the remnants of the resource base, where heightened aggressiveness would favor a spread of the viral agent among this residual rodent population. Following improved climatic conditions, the rodents may have invaded both farm fields and homes, where people were infected through aspiration of excreta, thereby initiating the cocoliztli epidemic. The native people of Mexico may have been preferentially infected because they worked the agricultural fields and facilities that were presumably infested with infected rodents.

Salmonella enterica—subset Paratyphi C to be exact—was present in the DNA of ten different individuals buried at the only known burial site, Teposcolula-Yucundaa, associated with cocoliztli.

According to study author Åshild Vågene from the Max Planck Institute, the strain is a bacterial infection that causes a type of enteric fever nearly identical to typhoid. While that specific strain of salmonella is much rarer today, Vågene says it would have spread similarly. Any food or water contaminated with the strain would have turned deadly once ingested.

Victims would have experienced a fever, vomiting, and likely a rash.

Ten lesser epidemics of cocoliztli began in the years 1559, 1566, 1587, 1592, 1601, 1604, 1606, 1613, 1624, and 1642. Nine of them began in years in which the tree-ring reconstructions of precipitation indicate winter-spring (November-March) and early summer (May-June) drought. But the worst epidemic of cocoliztli ever witnessed, 1545-1548, actually began during a brief wet episode within the era of prolonged drought. This pattern of drought followed by wetness associated with the 1545 epidemic is very similar to the dry-then-wet conditions associated with the hantavirus outbreak in 1993 when abundant rains after a long drought resulted in a tenfold increase in local deer mouse populations. Wet conditions during the year of epidemic outbreak in both 1545 and 1993 may have led to improved ecologic conditions and may also have resulted in a proliferation of rodents across the landscape and aggravated the cocoliztli epidemic of 1545-1548.

The cocoliztli epidemic, or the great pestilence, is a term given to millions of deaths in the territory of New Spain in present-day Mexico in the 16th century attributed to one or more illnesses collectively called cocoliztli, a mysterious illness characterized by high fevers and bleeding. It ravaged the Mexican highlands in epidemic proportions. The disease became known as Cocoliztli by the native Aztecs, and had devastating effects on the area's demography, particularly for the indigenous people.

The disease described by Dr. Hernandez in 1576 is difficult to link to any specific etiologic agent or disease known today. Some aspects of cocoliztli epidemiology suggest that a native agent hosted in a rain-sensitive rodent reservoir was responsible for the disease. Many of the symptoms described by Dr. Hernandez occur to a degree in infections by rodent-borne South American arenaviruses, but no arenavirus has been positively identified in Mexico. Hantavirus is a less likely candidate for cocoliztli because epidemics of severe hantavirus hemorrhagic fevers with high death rates are unknown in the New World. The hypothesized viral agent responsible for cocoliztli remains to be identified, but several new arenaviruses and hantaviruses have recently been isolated from the Americas and perhaps more remain to be discovered. If not extinct, the microorganism that caused cocoliztli may remain hidden in the highlands of Mexico and under favorable climatic conditions could reappear.

Based on the death toll, this outbreak is often referred to as the worst disease epidemic in the history of Mexico. Subsequent outbreaks continued to baffle both Spanish and native doctors, with little consensus among modern researchers on the pathogenesis. However, recent bacterial genomic studies have suggested that Salmonella, specifically a serotype of Salmonella enterica known as Paratyphi C, was at least partially responsible for this initial outbreak. It might have also been an indigenous viral hemorrhagic fever, perhaps exacerbated by the worst droughts to affect that region in 500 years, as well as living conditions for indigenous peoples of Mexico in the wake of the Spanish conquest (c. 1519).

The infection that caused the cocoliztli epidemic was a form of viral hemorrhagic fever that killed 15 million inhabitants of Mexico and Central America. Among a population already weakened by extreme drought, the disease proved to be utterly catastrophic. "Cocoliztli" is the Aztec word for "pest."

A recent study that examined DNA from the skeletons of victims found that they were infected with a subspecies of Salmonella known as S. paratyphi C, which causes enteric fever, a category of fever that includes typhoid. Enteric fever can cause high fever, dehydration, and gastrointestinal problems and is still a major health threat today.

HISTORY

There have been 12 epidemics that have been identified as potentially being of cocoliztli, with the largest ones being those in 1520, 1545, 1576, 1736, and 1813. Soto et al. have hypothesized that a large-scale outbreak of hemorrhagic fever could also have contributed to the earlier collapse of the Classic Mayan civilization (AD 750–950), though most experts believe other factors including climate change likely played a much larger role.

Cocoliztli epidemics usually occurred within two years of a major drought, while another disease called "matlazahuatl" appeared within two years of rainy periods. The epidemic in 1576 occurred after a drought stretching from Venezuela to Canada. The correlation between drought and the disease has been thought to be that population numbers of the vesper mouse, a carrier of viral hemorrhagic fever, increased during the rains that followed the drought, as conditions improved.

There exists some ambiguity regarding if cocoliztli preferentially targeted native people, as opposed to European colonists. The majority of firsthand accounts regarding the outbreak come from Aztec informants, who were primarily concerned with the diseases' novelty and pronounced symptoms. Spanish colonizers may have used indigenous fears to further justify and enforce Christianity, as expressed by the following statement from Gonzalo de Ortiz (an encomendero): "envió Dios tal enfermedad Sobre Ellos Que de quarto partes de Indios que Avia se llevó las tres" (God sent down such sickness upon the Indians that three out of every four of them perished). It is unclear if Ortiz was exaggerating, or if the Spanish colonizers were truly less affected by this "act of God". Accounts by Toribio de Benavente Motolinia, an early Spanish missionary, seem to contradict Ortiz's sentiment by suggesting that 60–90% of New Spain's total population decreased, regardless of ethnicity. Bernardino de Sahagún, another Spanish clergyman and author of the Florentine Codex, attested to contracting the disease himself towards the end of the outbreak. During a second cocoliztli outbreak in 1576, Sahagún identified both African slaves and Spanish colonists as being susceptible to the disease.

SOURCES AND VECTORS

The social and physical environment of Colonial Mexico was likely key in allowing the Outbreak of 1545–1548 to reach the heights that it did. Already weakened by war and earlier disease outbreaks, the Aztecs were forced into easily governable reducciones (congregations) that focused on agricultural production and conversion to Christianity. The reducciones would have not only brought people in much closer contact with one another but with animals, as well. Whether it is rats, chickens, pigs, or cattle, animals imported from the Old World were potentially disease vectors for illnesses of New and Old World origins.

At the same time, droughts plagued Central America, with tree-ring data showing that the outbreak occurred amid a megadrought. The lack of water would have altered sanitary conditions and encouraged poor hygiene habits. Megadroughts were reported before both the 1545 and 1576 outbreaks. Additionally, periodic rains during a supposed megadrought, such as those hypothesized for shortly before 1545, would have increased the presence of New World rats and mice. These animals are believed to have also been able to transport the arenaviruses capable of causing hemorrhagic fevers. The effects of drought, combined with the now crowded settlements, is a highly plausible explanation for disease transmission, especially if the pathogens are spread by either human fecal matter or animals.

The Aztecs and other indigenous groups affected by the outbreak were potentially put at a disadvantage given their lack of exposure to zoonotic diseases. Given that many of the Old World pathogens are considered responsible for the cocoliztli outbreak, it is significant that all but one of the most common species of domestic mammalian livestock (llamas/alpacas being the exception) come from the Old World.

EXTENT

Scholars suspect it began in the southern and central Mexico Highlands, near modern-day Puebla City. Shortly after its initial onset, however, it may have spread as far north as Sinaloa, and as south as Chiapas and Guatemala, where it was called gucumatz. It may have even crossed the South American border, and into Ecuador and Peru, although it is hard to be certain that the same disease was described. The outbreak seemed to be limited to a higher elevation, as it was nearly absent from coastal regions at sea level, e.g. the plains along the Gulf of Mexico and Pacific coast.

SYMPTOMS

The symptoms were unlike anything the doctors of the time had seen. Victims turned yellow from jaundice, and blood ran from their ears and noses. They had hallucinations and agonizing convulsions. They died in days. Aztecs called it the cocoliztli, meaning pestilence in the local Nahuatl language. "The cocoliztli appeared from almost nowhere. Nobody knew what it was," says Rodolfo Acuña-Soto, a historical epidemiologist at the National Autonomous University of Mexico in Mexico City.

Although symptomatic descriptions of cocoliztli are similar to those of Old World diseases (e.g. measles, yellow fever, typhus), many researchers believe that it should be recognized as a separate disease. According to Francisco Hernández de Toledo, a physician who witnessed the outbreak in 1576, symptoms included high fever, severe headache, vertigo, black tongue, dark urine, dysentery, severe abdominal and chest pain, head and neck nodules, neurologic disorders, jaundice, and profuse bleeding from the nose, eyes, and mouth; death frequently occurred within 3 to 4 days. Some also describe the afflicted during this period as having spotted skin and gastrointestinal hemorrhaging, leading to bloody diarrhea, as well as bleeding from the eyes, mouth, and vagina. The onset was often rapid, and without any precursors that would suggest one was sick. The disease was characterized by an extremely high level of virulence, with death often occurring within a week of one becoming symptomatic. Due to the virulence and effectiveness of the disease, recognizing its existence in the archaeological record has been difficult. Cocoliztli, and other diseases that work rapidly, usually do not leave impacts (lesions) on the decedent's bones, despite causing significant damage to the gastrointestinal, respiratory, and other bodily systems.

CAUSES

Even today, nobody knows what exactly was responsible for the epidemic, which first appeared in Mexico, then called New Spain, in the 16th century and killed an estimated 45% of the entire native population. Historical records suggest it was some type of hemorrhagic fever—like Ebola—but DNA evidence published this week suggests the culprit might have been salmonella—a common food-borne illness—brought by European colonizers.

Numerous 16th-century accounts detail the outbreak's devastation, but the symptoms do not match any known pathogen. Shortly after 1548, the Spanish started calling the disease tabardillo (typhus), which had only been recognized in Spain since the late 15th century. However, the symptoms of cocoliztli were still not identical to the typhus, or spotted fever, observed in the Old World at that time. Perhaps, this is why Francisco Hernández de Toledo, a Spanish physician, insisted on using the Nahuatl word when describing the disease to correspondents in the Old World. Centuries later, in 1970, a historian named Germain Somolinos d'Ardois took a systematic look at all the proposed explanations at the time, including hemorrhagic influenza, leptospirosis, malaria, typhus, typhoid, and yellow fever. According to Somolinos d'Amboise, none of these quite matched the 16th-century accounts of cocoliztli, leading him to conclude the disease was a result of the "viral process of hemorrhagic influence." In other words, Somolinos d'Ardois believed cocoliztli was not the result of any known Old World pathogen, but possibly, a virus of either European or New World origins.

The evidence was tucked in the teeth of 29 skeletons unearthed from the ruins of an ancient city archaeologists call Teposcolula Yucundaa in the Oaxaca region of Mexico. The main inhabitants were the Mixtec people, a distinct group from the Aztecs of central Mexico. Twenty-four skeletons came from a cemetery dating to the first cocoliztli outbreak in 1545, and five came from a cemetery roughly 100 years older. Pathogens that ravaged the body at its death can be entombed within the tooth's inner chamber and detected years later, says Kirsten Bos, a molecular paleobiologist at the Max Planck Institute for the Science of Human History in Jena, Germany, and an author on the study.

It's harder to tell whether the salmonella alone killed these people, Poinar says. "I'm buying that it likely contributed to this epidemic. Is that what they died of? I'd be careful of saying that." Perhaps salmonella was simply one of the multiple infections that together became deadlier and caused cocoliztli, he says.

Historical descriptions of the cocoliztli certainly don't sound like salmonella, Acuña-Soto says. "The paper is great. We [now] know there's an outbreak of salmonella," he says. "But never in history have I heard of salmonella doing something like cocoliztli with the bleeding, jaundice, the spread."

But Bos thinks salmonella still might be behind the cocoliztli, saying that for her team to detect the pathogen, these people must have had "massive" amounts of the bacteria in their blood. "When you get a very advanced bacterial infection, you can get bleeding from orifices and symptoms very similar to a hemorrhagic fever," she says. "The historical records match a hemorrhagic fever, but we shouldn't be too dismissive on what biologic agent it was."

It's difficult to say why the cocoliztli was so deadly for the native peoples, but the indigenous population may also have been suffering from malnourishment as a result of a great drought that afflicted the region at the time, Acuña-Soto says.

If the bug wasn't present in the Americas before European arrival, the locals may have lacked a strong natural immune response to the disease and made them more susceptible. Whatever the pathogen, it swept through the region like a storm. At the time, historian Fray Juan de Torquemada wrote, "In the year 1576, a great mortality and pestilence that lasted for more than a year overcame the Indians ... the place we know as New Spain was left almost empty."

It has been speculated that it might have been an indigenous viral hemorrhagic fever as there are accounts of similar diseases having struck Mexico in Precolumbian times. The Codex Chimalpopoca states that an outbreak of bloody diarrhea occurred in Colhuacan in 1320. If the disease was indigenous, it was perhaps exacerbated by the worst droughts to affect that region in 500 years and living conditions for indigenous peoples of Mexico in the wake of the Spanish conquest (c. 1519). Some historians have suggested it was typhus, measles, or smallpox, though the symptoms did not match.

Marr and Kiracofe (2000) attempted to build off this work by reexamining Hernandez's account of cocoliztli and comparing them with various clinical descriptions of other diseases. They suggested that scholars consider "New World arenaviruses" and the role these pathogens may have played in colonial disease outbreaks. Rebelling against the universal acceptance of Post-Contact epidemics being "Old-World importations," Marr and Kiracofe theorized that arenaviruses, which mainly affect rodents, were largely kept away from Pre-Columbian people. Consequently, rat and mice infestations brought upon by the arrival of the Spanish may combine with climatic and landscape change, which have brought these arenaviruses into much closer contact with people. Subsequent studies seemed to have accepted the viral hemorrhagic fever diagnosis and became more interested in assessing how the disease became so widespread.

In 2018, Johannes Krause, an evolutionary geneticist at the Max Planck Institute for the Science of Human History, and colleagues discovered new evidence for an Old World culprit. DNA samples from the teeth of 29 sixteenth-century skeletons in the Oaxaca region of Mexico were identified as belonging to a rare strain of the bacterium Salmonella enterica (subs. enterica) which causes paratyphoid fever, suggesting that paratyphoid was the underlying fever behind the disease.

The team extracted ancient DNA from the teeth of 29 individuals buried at Teposcolula-Yucundaa in Oaxaca, Mexico. The Contact-era site has the only cemetery to be conclusively linked to victims of the Cocoliztli Outbreak of 1545–1548. Using the MEGAN alignment tool (MALT), a program that attempts to match fragments of extracted DNA with a database of bacterial genomes, the researchers were able to recognize nonlocal microbial infections.

Within 10 individuals, they identified Salmonella enterica subsp. enterica serovar Paratyphi C, which causes enteric fevers in humans. This strain of Salmonella is unique to humans and was not found in any soil samples or pre-Contact individuals that were used as controls. Enteric fevers, also known as typhoid or paratyphoid, are similar to typhus and were only distinguished from one another in the 19th century. Today, S. Paratyphi C continues to cause enteric fevers, and if untreated, has a mortality rate up to 15%. Infections are largely limited to developing nations in Africa and Asia, although enteric fevers, in general, are still a health threat worldwide. Infections with S. Paratyphi C are rare, as the majority of cases reported (about 27 million in 2000) were the result of the serovars S. Typhi and S. Paratyphi A.

These findings are boosted by the recent discovery of S. Paratyphi C within a 13th-century Norwegian cemetery. A young female, who likely died from enteric fever, is proof that the pathogen was present in Europe over 300 years before the epidemics in Mexico. Thus, it is possible that healthy carriers transported the bacteria to the New World, where it thrived. Those who unknowingly possessed the bacteria were likely aided from generations of contact with it, as it is believed that S. Paratyphi C may have first transferred over to humans from swine in the Old World during, or, shortly after the Neolithic period.

Some, including an evolutionary geneticist, María Ávila-Arcos, have questioned this evidence since S. Centrica's symptoms are poorly matched with the disease. Both Ávila-Arcos, and even Krause's team and authors of earlier historical analyses, point out that RNA viruses, among other non-bacterial pathogens, had not been investigated. Others have highlighted the fact that certain symptoms described, including gastrointestinal hemorrhaging, are not present in current observations of S. Paratyphi C infections. Ultimately, a more definitive proposal for the cause of any of the cocoliztli epidemics of 1545–1548 and 1576-81 awaits further developments in ancient RNA analysis and the causes of different outbreaks may prove to differ.

Historians and archaeologists have long suspected that a blood-borne illness was responsible for cocoliztli. Depictions by both Spanish and indigenous artists show the infected with nose bleeds and coughing up blood.

Direct physical evidence, however, has been hard to find.

"This is one of the diseases that doesn't leave any visible clues on the skeleton," says Vågene, adding that very few diseases do.

So, to detect the presence of a pathogen, researchers instead turned to 500-year-old DNA embedded in the teeth of 24 indigenous individuals' remains.

Scientists ran the samples through a DNA sequencing analysis called MALT, a computational program that stores information from all known and characterized pathogens.

"One of the most important aspects is we didn't need to make any assumptions," says Alexander Herbig, also from Max Planck and another author on the study. Instead of forming a hypothesis for several different pathogens, researchers could instead test the DNA against the huge swath in their database.

Of the 24 that were tested, 10 showed signs of salmonella. In addition to testing individuals that had contact with Europeans, the researchers also tested five individuals that had been buried before Europeans arrived. None of those five had DNA evidence of salmonella.

When Europeans entered the Americas, historical records show they brought several infectious diseases with them, including smallpox and measles. These diseases disproportionately impacted native people—because they didn't have immunity to them.

Vågene and Herbig say their working hypothesis is that the same was true when the Spanish landed in Mexico.

In a study published in February of last year, researchers noted that this same strain of salmonella was detected in the DNA remains of a Norwegian woman who died in 1200. This means the specific strain that may have killed Aztecs in the 16th century had been present 300 years earlier across the Atlantic.

It's possible, says Vågene, that the pathogen had already been in Mexico. But such evidence has not been found.

To confirm that salmonella contributed to the historical outbreak in Mexico, scientists would need to test more DNA from different sites.

"From a gut instinct I would suspect there were multiple agents involved in that epidemic," says Caitlin Pepperrell, a researcher who studies infectious diseases at the University of Wisconsin-Madison who was not involved with the study.

Pepperrell says several other factors could have been at work, many stemming from consequences of colonialism, including "disruptions in food supplies, famine, changes in the concentrations of populations, and relocation."

"It is hard to know for sure," says Anne Stone of Arizona State University's School of Evolution and Social Change, who was also not involved in the study. "But I think that it likely was of European origin because it was new to the population and it hit them so hard."

She says that more DNA samples from more burial sites could confirm this theory.

Vågene agrees that until archaeologists identify more cocoliztli sites, researchers can only hypothesize what caused the massive outbreak. In the meantime, Herbig adds, they'll continue using DNA sequencing to find out what major diseases have impacted human history and how.

EFFECTS

DEATH TOLL

Beyond the estimations done by Motolinia and others for New Spain, most of the death toll figures cited for the outbreak of 1545–1548 are concerned with Aztec populations. Around 800,000 died in the Valley of Mexico, which led to the widespread abandonment of many indigenous sites in the area during, or, shortly after these four years. Estimates for the entire number of human lives lost during this epidemic have ranged from 5 to 15 million people, making it one of the most deadly disease outbreaks of all time.

OTHER

The effects of the outbreak extended beyond just a loss in terms of population. The lack of indigenous labor led to a sizeable food shortage, which affected both the natives and the Spanish. The death of many Aztecs due to the plague led to a void in land ownership, with Spanish colonists of all backgrounds looking to exploit these now vacant lands. Coincidentally, the Spanish Emperor, Charles V, had been seeking a way to disempower the encomendero class and establish a more efficient and "ethical" settlement system.

Starting around the end of the outbreak in 1549, the encoders, crippled by the loss in profits resulting and unable to meet the demands of New Spain, were forced to comply with the new tasaciones (regulations). The new ordinances, known as Leyes Nuevas aimed to limit the number of tribute encomenderos could personally extract, while also prohibiting them from exercising absolute control over the labor force. Simultaneously, non-encomenderos began claiming lands lost by the encomenderos, as well as, the labor provided by the indigenous. This developed into the implementation of the repartimiento system, which sought to institute a higher level of oversight within the Spanish colonies and maximize the overall tribute extracted for public and crown use. Rules regarding tribute itself were also changed in response to the epidemic of 1545, as fears over future food shortages ran rampant among the Spanish. By 1577, after years of debate and a second major outbreak of cocoliztli, maize and money was designated as the only two forms of acceptable tribute.

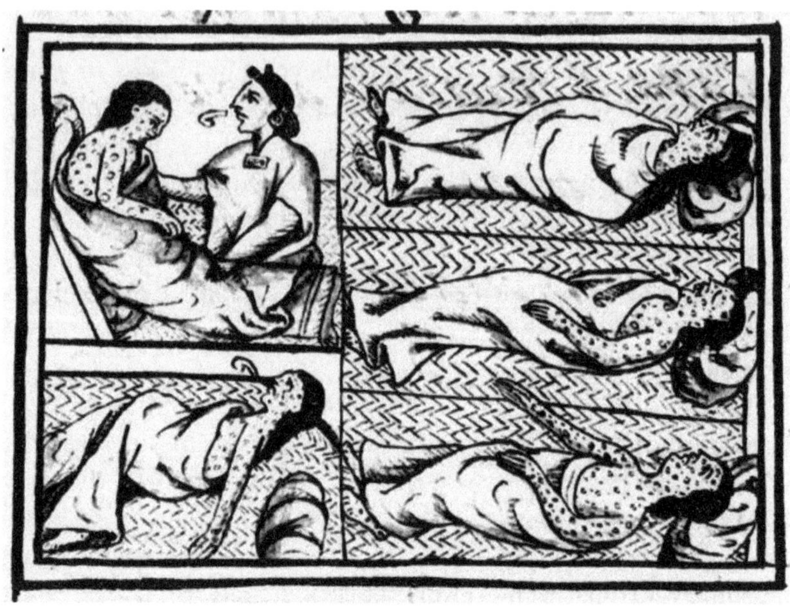

Fig. 4.1 Cocoliztli Epidemic

CHAPTER FIVE

THE ZIKA VIRUS EPIDEMIC

Zika virus is a member of the virus family Flaviviridae. It is spread by daytime-active Aedes mosquitoes, such as A. aegypti and A. albopictus. Its name comes from the Ziika Forest of Uganda, where the virus was first isolated in 1947. Zika virus shares a genus with dengue, yellow fever, Japanese encephalitis, and West Nile viruses. Since the 1950s, it has been known to occur within a narrow equatorial belt from Africa to Asia. From 2007 to 2016, the virus spread eastward, across the Pacific Ocean to the Americas, leading to the 2015–2016 Zika virus epidemic.

The Zika virus is most often spread to people through mosquito bites, primarily in tropical and subtropical areas of the world. Most people infected with the Zika virus have no signs or symptoms. Some people have a mild fever, rash, and muscle pain. In rare cases, the Zika virus may cause brain or nervous system complications, such as Guillain-Barre syndrome, even in people who never show symptoms of infection. Infection with the Zika virus is also called Zika, Zika fever, or Zika virus disease.

Women who are infected with the Zika virus during pregnancy have an increased risk of miscarriage. Zika virus infection during pregnancy also increases the risk of serious birth defects in infants, including a potentially fatal brain condition called microcephaly.

Researchers are working on a vaccine for the Zika virus. For now, the best way to prevent infection is to avoid mosquito bites and reduce mosquito habitats.

The infection, known as Zika fever or Zika virus disease, often causes no or only mild symptoms, similar to a very mild form of dengue fever. While there is no specific treatment, paracetamol (acetaminophen) and rest may help with the symptoms. As of April 2019, no vaccines have been approved for clinical use, however, several vaccines are currently in clinical trials. Zika can spread from a pregnant woman to her baby. This can result in microcephaly, severe brain malformations, and other birth defects. Zika infections in adults may result rarely in Guillain–Barré syndrome.

In January 2016, the United States Centers for Disease Control and Prevention (CDC) issued travel guidance on affected countries, including the use of enhanced precautions, and guidelines for pregnant women including considering postponing travel. Other governments or health agencies also issued similar travel warnings, while Colombia, the Dominican Republic, Puerto Rico, Ecuador, El Salvador, and Jamaica advised women to postpone getting pregnant until more is known about the risks.

An epidemic of Zika fever, caused by the Zika virus, began in Brazil and affected other countries in the Americas from April 2015 to November 2016. The World Health Organization (WHO) declared the end of the epidemic in November 2016, but noted that the virus still represents "a highly significant and long term problem". It is estimated that 1.5 million people were infected by the Zika virus in Brazil, with over 3,500 cases of infant microcephaly reported between October 2015 and January 2016. The epidemic also affected other parts of South and North America, as well as several islands in the Pacific.

Zika virus spread to Brazil from Oceania in 2013 or 2014. Brazil notified the WHO of an illness characterized by skin rash in March 2015, and Zika was identified as the cause in May 2015. In February 2016, the WHO declared the outbreak a Public Health Emergency of International Concern as evidence grew that Zika can cause birth defects as well as neurological problems. The virus can be transmitted from a pregnant woman to her fetus and can cause microcephaly and other severe brain anomalies in the infant. Zika infections in adults can result in Guillain–Barré syndrome. In approximately one in five cases, Zika virus infections result in Zika fever, a minor illness that causes symptoms such as fever and a rash. Before the outbreak, Zika was considered a mild infection, as most infections are asymptomatic, making it difficult to determine precise estimates of the number of cases.

The virus is spread mainly by the Aedes aegypti mosquito, which is commonly found throughout the tropical and subtropical Americas. It can also be spread by the Aedes albopictus ("Asian tiger") mosquito, which is distributed as far north as the Great Lakes region in North America. People infected with Zika can transmit the virus to their sexual partners.

Several countries were issued travel warnings, and the outbreak was expected to reduce tourism significantly. Several countries took the unusual step of advising their citizens to delay pregnancy until more was known about the virus and its impact on fetal development. Furthermore, the outbreak raised concerns regarding the safety of athletes and spectators at the 2016 Summer Olympics and Paralympics in Rio de Janeiro.

VIROLOGY

Zika virus belongs to the family Flaviviridae and the genus Flavivirus, this is related to the dengue, yellow fever, Japanese encephalitis, and West Nile viruses. Like other flaviviruses, the Zika virus is enveloped and icosahedral and has a nonsegmented, single-stranded, 10 kilobase, positive-sense RNA genome. It is most closely related to the Spondweni virus and is one of the two known viruses in the Spondweni virus clade.

A positive-sense RNA genome can be directly translated into viral proteins. As in other flaviviruses, such as the similarly sized West Nile virus, the RNA genome encodes seven nonstructural proteins and three structural proteins in the form of a single polyprotein (Q32ZE1). One of the structural proteins encapsulates the virus. This protein is the flavivirus envelope glycoprotein, that binds to the endosomal membrane of the host cell to initiate endocytosis. The RNA genome forms a nucleocapsid along with copies of the 12-kDa capsid protein. The nucleocapsid, in turn, is enveloped within a host-derived membrane modified with two viral glycoproteins. Viral genome replication depends on the making of double-stranded RNA from the single-stranded, positive-sense RNA (ssRNA(+)) genome followed by transcription and replication to provide viral mRNAs and new ssRNA(+) genomes.

A longitudinal study shows that 6 hours after cells are infected with the Zika virus, the vacuoles and mitochondria in the cells begin to swell. This swelling becomes so severe, it results in cell death, also known as paraptosis. This form of programmed cell death requires gene expression. IFITM3 is a transmembrane protein in a cell that can protect it from viral infection by blocking virus attachment. Cells are most susceptible to Zika infection when levels of IFITM3 are low. Once the cell has been infected, the virus restructures the endoplasmic reticulum, forming the large vacuoles, resulting in cell death.

There are two Zika lineages: the African lineage and the Asian lineage. Phylogenetic studies indicate that the virus spreading in the Americas is 89% identical to African genotypes, but is most closely related to the Asian strain that circulated in French Polynesia during the 2013–2014 outbreak. The Asian strain appears to have first evolved around 1928.

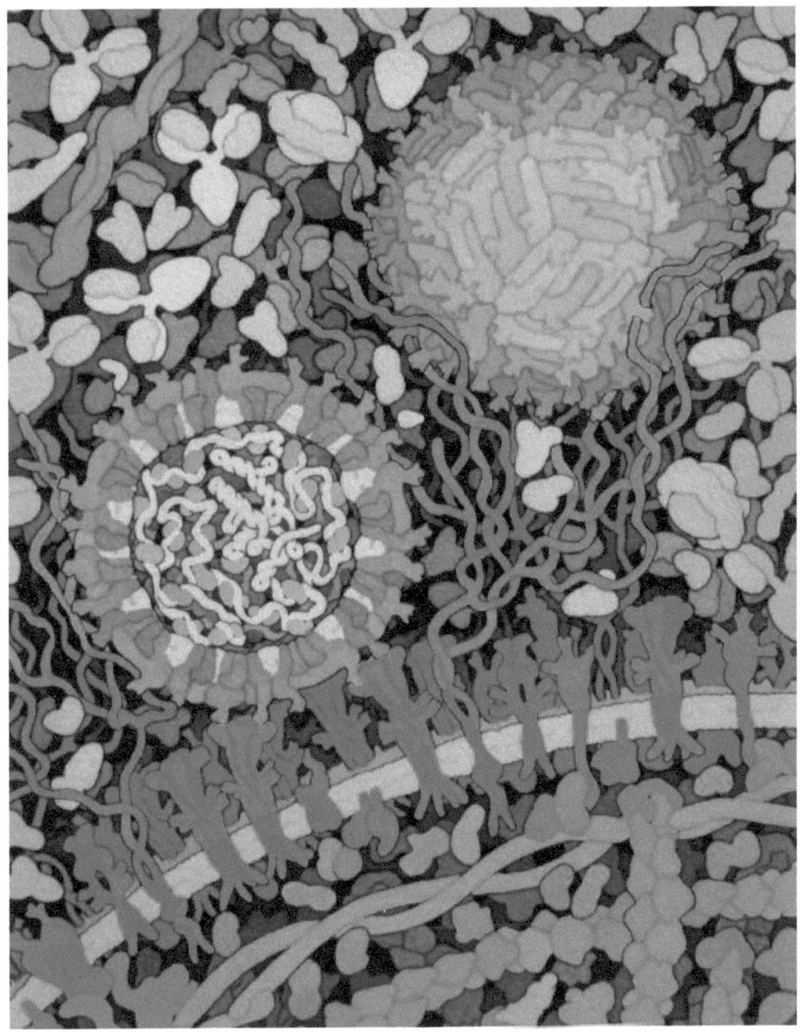

Fig. 5.1 Cross Section of Zika Virus

EPIDEMIOLOGY

As early as August 2014, physicians in Natal, in northeastern Brazil began to investigate an outbreak of illness characterized by a flat pinkish rash, bloodshot eyes, fever, joint pain, and headaches. While the symptoms resembled dengue fever, testing ruled out this and several other potential causes. By March 2015, the illness had spread to Salvador, Bahia, and had appeared in three different states. Then, in May 2015, researchers from the Federal University of Bahia and the Evandro Chagas Institute determined, using the RT-PCR technique, that the illness was an outbreak of the Zika virus. Although, the first confirmed Zika virus infection in Brazil was diagnosed by a returning traveler in March 2015.

The Zika virus was first isolated in 1947, in a rhesus monkey in a forest near Entebbe, Uganda. Although serologic evidence indicated additional human exposure during subsequent decades in parts of Africa and Asia, before the 2007 Yap Islands Zika virus outbreak, only 14 cases of human Zika virus disease had been documented.

Researchers generally believe the virus was brought to Brazil by an infected traveler who had been exposed to the virus in French Polynesia, who was then bitten by a mosquito that then infected others. Phylogenetic analysis of the first Brazilian infections has strongly indicated that the circulating virus is the Asian, rather than African, a strain of the virus, and was genetically similar to the virus found in the outbreak in French Polynesia. It appears Zika's route – from Africa and Asia to Oceania and then the Americas – may mirror that of chikungunya and dengue, both of which are now endemic in a large portion of the Americas.

The specific event that brought the virus to Brazil was uncertain until March 2016. Brazilian researchers had suggested that the Zika virus arrived during the 2014 FIFA World Cup tournament. French researchers speculated the virus arrived shortly afterward, in August 2014, when canoeing teams from French Polynesia, New Caledonia, Easter Island, and the Cook Islands, which had been or were experiencing Zika outbreaks, attended the Va'a World Sprint Championships in Rio de Janeiro. However, the outbreak in French Polynesia is known to have peaked and declined precipitously by

February 2014, lending doubt to the suggestion the virus arrived later that year in Brazil with spectators and competitors. In March 2016, a study published in Science, which developed a "molecular clock" based on the count of virus mutations in a relatively small sample, suggested Zika virus arrived in the Americas (most likely in Brazil) from French Polynesia between May and December 2013, well before the World Cup and Va'a Championships. In the Science article, Faria and colleagues managed to trace the origins of the virus strain that is circulating in Brazil and found that this strain has little genetic variability when compared to the strain of French Polynesia; after relating the number of travelers arriving in Brazil from French Polynesia with the cases reported and the events happening in that year, the team was able to deduce that the virus arrived in Brazil in 2013 during the Confederation Cup, when Tahiti's team played against other teams in a few Brazilian cities, which attracted many tourists from both places. Zika virus usually has very mild, or no symptoms, so it took almost a year for Brazil to confirm the first case of the disease. By then the outbreak was already widespread. Factors associated with the rapid spread of the Zika virus in Brazil include the non-immune population, high population density, tropical climate, and inadequate control of Aedes mosquitoes in the country. The Zika virus epidemic also revealed structural problems of the health system, in particular in public health services and basic sanitation in Brazil.

The above-average warm temperatures of 2015–2016 caused by a strong El Nino created an environment conducive to the spread of the Zika Virus in Brazil. The 2015 -16 El Nino increased ocean and ground surface temperatures to above average. January 2016 brought about nine consecutive months with temperatures 1.04 °C above the global average. It is important to note, however, that while South America had areas experiencing 2.0 °C above-average temperatures (for 1981–2010), areas including Argentina, Southern Brazil, and Uruguay experienced temperatures 0.5 °C below average.

Precipitation is another crucial factor to consider as Eastern Brazil and other areas in southern South America experienced high amounts of precipitation in early 2016. The environmental conditions of increased rainfall and higher average temperatures in the South American region, lead to both a longer mosquito season and a higher mosquito density which created an environment in which the Zika carrying Aedes aegypti and Aedes albopictus mosquitoes can thrive. Looking forward, climate models suggest that regions favorable to the Aedes mosquitoes will grow, widening the range of Zika and other mosquito-carried diseases. The potential for epidemics will spread inland and into other regions of the world, not just in the tropical environment.

SYMPTOMS

As many as 4 out of 5 people infected with the Zika virus have no signs or symptoms. When symptoms do occur, they usually begin two to 14 days after a person is bitten by an infected mosquito. Symptoms usually last about a week, and most people recover fully.

Signs and symptoms of the Zika virus most commonly include:

Mild fever, Rash, Joint pain, particularly in the hands or feet, Red eyes (conjunctivitis).

Other signs and symptoms may include:

Muscle pain, Headache, Eye pain, Fatigue or a general feeling of discomfort, Abdominal pain.

COMPLICATIONS

Women who are infected with the Zika virus during pregnancy have an increased risk of miscarriage, preterm birth, and stillbirth. Zika virus infection during pregnancy also increases the risk of serious birth defects in infants (congenital Zika syndrome), including:

A much smaller than the normal brain and head size (microcephaly), with a partly collapsed skull

Brain damage and reduced brain tissue

Eye damage

Joint problems, including limited motion

Reduced body movement due to too much muscle tone after birth

In adults, infection with the Zika virus may cause brain or nervous system complications, such as Guillain-Barre syndrome, even in people who never show symptoms of infection.

Zika virus infection during pregnancy is a cause of microcephaly and other congenital abnormalities in the developing fetus and newborn. Zika infection in pregnancy also results in pregnancy complications such as fetal loss, stillbirth, and preterm birth.

Zika virus infection is also a trigger of Guillain-Barré syndrome, neuropathy, and myelitis, particularly in adults and older children.

Research is ongoing to investigate the effects of Zika virus infection on pregnancy outcomes, strategies for prevention and control, and effects of infection on other neurological disorders in children and adults.

PREVENTION

If you are living in or traveling to areas where the Zika virus is known to be, take steps to reduce your risk of mosquito bites:

Stay in air-conditioned or well-screened housing. The mosquitoes that carry the Zika virus are most active from dawn to dusk, but they can also bite at night. Consider sleeping under a mosquito bed net, especially if you are outside.

Wear protective clothing. When you go into mosquito-infested areas, wear a long sleeved shirt, long pants, socks, and shoes.

Use insect repellent. You can apply permethrin to your clothing, shoes, camping gear, and bed netting. You can also buy clothing made with permethrin already in it. For your skin, use a repellent that contains DEET, picaridin, or one of the other active ingredients registered with the Environmental Protection Agency and known to be effective against mosquitoes. When used as directed, these repellents are proven safe and effective, even for pregnant and breastfeeding women.

Reduce mosquito habitat. The mosquitoes that carry the Zika virus usually live in and around houses and breed in standing water that has collected in containers such as animal dishes, flower pots, and used automobile tires. At least once a week, empty any sources of standing water to help lower mosquito populations.

ZIKA VIRUS AND BLOOD DONATION

In some cases, the Zika virus has spread from one person to another through blood products (blood transfusion). To reduce the risk of spread through blood transfusion, blood donation centers in the United States and its territories are required to screen all blood donations for the Zika virus. If you had Zika or if you live in the U.S. and recently traveled to an area where the Zika virus is widespread, your local blood donation center may recommend that you wait four weeks to donate blood.

TRANSMISSION

The vertebrate hosts of the virus were primarily monkeys in a so-called enzootic mosquito-monkey-mosquito cycle, with only occasional transmission to humans. Before the current pandemic began in 2007, Zika "rarely caused recognized 'spillover' infections in humans, even in highly enzootic areas". Infrequently, however, other arboviruses have become established as human diseases and spread in a mosquito–human–mosquito cycle, like the yellow fever virus and the dengue fever virus (both flaviviruses), and the chikungunya virus (a togavirus). Though the reason for the pandemic is unknown, dengue, a related arbovirus that infects the same species of mosquito vectors, is known in particular to be intensified by urbanization and globalization. Zika is primarily spread by Aedes aegypti mosquitoes, and can also be transmitted through sexual contact or blood transfusions. The basic reproduction number (R0, a measure of transmissibility) of the Zika virus has been estimated to be between 1.4 and 6.6.

In 2015, news reports drew attention to the rapid spread of Zika in Latin America and the Caribbean. At that time, the Pan American Health Organization published a list of countries and territories that experienced "local Zika virus transmission" comprising Barbados, Bolivia, Brazil, Colombia, the Dominican Republic, Ecuador, El Salvador, French Guiana, Guadeloupe, Guatemala, Guyana, Haiti, Honduras, Martinique, Mexico, Panama, Paraguay, Puerto Rico, Saint Martin, Suriname, and Venezuela. By August 2016, more than 50 countries had experienced active (local) transmission of the Zika virus.

MOSQUITO

Zika is primarily spread by the female Aedes aegypti mosquito, which is active mostly in the daytime. The mosquitos must feed on blood to lay eggs. The virus has also been isolated from several arboreal mosquito species in the genus Aedes, such as *A. Africanus, A. apicoargenteus, A. furcifer, A. hensilli, A. luteocephalus, and A. vittatus*, with an extrinsic incubation period in mosquitoes around 10 days.

The true extent of the vectors is still unknown. Zika has been detected in many more species of Aedes, along with Anopheles coustani, Mansonia uniformis, and Culex perfuscus, although this alone does not incriminate them as vectors. To detect the presence of the virus usually requires genetic material to be analyzed in a lab using the technique RT-PCR. A much cheaper and faster method involves shining a light at the head and thorax of the mosquito and detecting chemical compounds characteristic of the virus using near-infrared spectroscopy.

Transmission by A. albopictus, the tiger mosquito, was reported from a 2007 urban outbreak in Gabon, where it had newly invaded the country and become the primary vector for the concomitant chikungunya and dengue virus outbreaks. New outbreaks can occur if a person carrying the virus travels to another region where A. albopictus is common.

The potential societal risk of Zika can be delimited by the distribution of the mosquito species that transmit it. The global distribution of the most cited carrier of Zika, A. aegypti, is expanding due to global trade and travel. A. aegypti distribution is now the most extensive ever recorded – on parts of all continents except Antarctica, including North America and even the European periphery (Madeira, the Netherlands, and the northeastern Black Sea coast). A mosquito population capable of carrying Zika has been found in a Capitol Hill neighborhood of Washington, DC, and genetic evidence suggests they survived at least four consecutive winters in the region. The study authors conclude that mosquitos are adapting for persistence in a northern climate. Zika virus appears to be contagious via mosquitoes for around a week after infection. The virus is thought to be infectious for a long time after infection (at least 2 weeks) when transmitted via semen.

Research into its ecological niche suggests that Zika may be influenced to a greater degree by changes in precipitation and temperature than dengue, making it more likely to be confined to tropical areas. However, rising global temperatures would allow for the disease vector to expand its range further north, allowing Zika to follow.

BLOOD TRANSFUSION

As of April 2016, two cases of Zika transmission through blood transfusions have been reported globally, both from Brazil, after which the US Food and Drug Administration (FDA) recommended screening blood donors and deferring high-risk donors for 4 weeks. A potential risk had been suspected based on a blood-donor screening study during the French Polynesian Zika outbreak, in which 2.8% of donors from November 2013 and February 2014 tested positive for Zika RNA and were all asymptomatic at the time of blood donation. Eleven of the positive donors reported symptoms of Zika fever after their donation, but only three of 34 samples grew in culture.

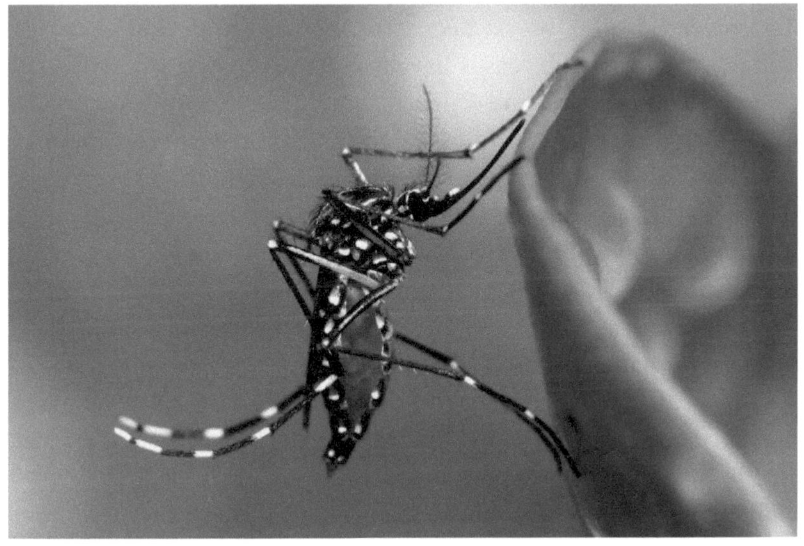

Fig. 5.2 Adult *Aedes aegypti* mosquito

PATHOGENESIS

Zika virus replicates in the mosquito's midgut epithelial cells and then its salivary gland cells. After 5–10 days, the virus can be found in the mosquito's saliva. If the mosquito's saliva is inoculated into human skin, the virus can infect epidermal keratinocytes, skin fibroblasts in the skin, and the Langerhans cells. The pathogenesis of the virus is hypothesized to continue with a spread to lymph nodes and the bloodstream. Flaviviruses replicate in the cytoplasm, but Zika antigens have been found in infected cell nuclei.

The viral protein numbered NS4A can lead to a small head size (microcephaly) because it disrupts brain growth by hijacking a pathway that regulates the growth of new neurons. In fruit flies, both NS4A and the neighboring NS4B restrict eye growth.

ZIKA FEVER

Zika fever (also known as Zika virus disease) is an illness caused by the Zika virus. Most cases have no symptoms, but when present they are usually mild and can resemble dengue fever. Symptoms may include fever, red eyes, joint pain, headache, and a maculopapular rash. Symptoms generally last less than seven days. It has not caused any reported deaths during the initial infection. Infection during pregnancy causes microcephaly and other brain malformations in some babies. Infection in adults has been linked to Guillain–Barré syndrome (GBS) and the Zika virus has been shown to infect human Schwann cells.

Diagnosis is by testing the blood, urine, or saliva for the presence of Zika virus RNA when the person is sick. In 2019, an improved diagnostic test, based on research from Washington University in St. Louis, that detects Zika infection in serum was granted market authorization by the FDA.

Prevention involves decreasing mosquito bites in areas where the disease occurs, and proper use of condoms. Efforts to prevent bites include the use of DEET or picaridin-based insect repellent, covering much of the body with clothing, mosquito nets, and getting rid of standing water where mosquitoes reproduce. There is no vaccine. Health officials recommended that women in areas affected by the 2015–2016 Zika outbreak consider putting off pregnancy and that pregnant women do not travel to these areas. While no specific treatment exists, paracetamol (acetaminophen) and rest may help with the symptoms. Admission to a hospital is rarely necessary.

VACCINE DEVELOPMENT

The World Health Organization has suggested that priority should be to develop inactivated vaccines and other non-live vaccines, which are safe to use in pregnant women.

As of March 2016, 18 companies and institutions were developing vaccines against Zika, but they state a vaccine is unlikely to be widely available for about 10 years.

In June 2016, the FDA granted the first approval for a human clinical trial for a Zika vaccine. In March 2017, a DNA vaccine was approved for phase-2 clinical trials. This vaccine consists of a small, circular piece of DNA, known as a plasmid, that expresses the genes for the Zika virus envelope proteins. As the vaccine does not contain the full sequence of the virus, it cannot cause infection. As of April 2017, both subunit and inactivated vaccines have entered clinical trials.

HISTORY

VIRUS ISOLATION IN MONKEYS AND MOSQUITOES, 1947

The virus was first isolated in April 1947 from a rhesus macaque monkey placed in a cage in the Ziika Forest of Uganda, near Lake Victoria, by the scientists of the Yellow Fever Research Institute. Second isolation from the mosquito A. Africanus followed at the same site in January 1948. When the monkey developed a fever, researchers isolated from its serum a "filterable transmissible agent" which was named Zika in 1948.

FIRST EVIDENCE OF HUMAN INFECTION, 1952

Zika was first known to infect humans from the results of a serological survey in Uganda, published in 1952. Of 99 human blood samples tested, 6.1% had neutralizing antibodies. As part of a 1954 outbreak investigation of jaundice suspected to be yellow fever, researchers reported the isolation of the virus from a patient, but the pathogen was later shown to be the closely related Spondweni virus. Spondweni was also determined to be the cause of a self-inflicted infection as a researcher reported in 1956.

SPREAD IN EQUATORIAL AFRICA AND ASIA

Subsequent serological studies in several African and Asian countries indicated the virus had been widespread within human populations in these regions. The first true case of human infection was identified by Simpson in 1964, who was himself infected while isolating the virus from mosquitoes. From then until 2007, there were only 13 further confirmed human cases of Zika infection from Africa and Southeast Asia. A study published in 2017 showed that the Zika virus, despite only a few cases were reported, has been silently circulated in West Africa for the last two decades when blood samples collected between 1992 and 2016 were tested for the ZIKV IgM antibodies.

MICRONESIA, 2007

In April 2007, the first outbreak outside of Africa and Asia occurred on the island of Yap in the Federated States of Micronesia, characterized by rash, conjunctivitis, and arthralgia, which was initially thought to be dengue, chikungunya, or Ross River disease. Serum samples from patients in the acute phase of illness contained RNA of Zika. There were 49 confirmed cases, 59 unconfirmed cases, no hospitalizations, and no deaths.

2013-2014

After October 2013 Oceania's first outbreak showed an estimated 11% population infected for French Polynesia that also presented with Guillain–Barre syndrome (GBS). The spread of ZIKV continued to New Caledonia, Easter Island, and the Cook Islands where 1385 cases were confirmed by January 2014. During the same year, Easter Island acknowledged 51 cases. Australia began seeing cases in 2012. Research showed it was brought by travelers returning from Indonesia and other infected countries. New Zealand also experienced an infections rate increase through returning foreign travelers. Oceania countries experiencing Zika today are New Caledonia, Vanuatu, Solomon Islands, Marshall Islands, American Samoa, Samoa, and Tonga.

Between 2013 and 2014, further epidemics occurred in French Polynesia, Easter Island, the Cook Islands, and New Caledonia

AMERICA

There was an epidemic in 2015 and 2016 in the Americas. The outbreak began in April 2015 in Brazil and spread to other countries in South America, Central America, North America, and the Caribbean. In January 2016, the WHO said the virus was likely to spread throughout most of the Americas by the end of the year; and in February 2016, the WHO declared the cluster of microcephaly and Guillain–Barré syndrome cases reported in Brazil – strongly suspected to be associated with the Zika outbreak – a Public Health Emergency of International Concern. It was estimated that 1.5 million people were infected by Zika in Brazil, with over 3,500 cases of microcephaly reported between October 2015 and January 2016.

Several countries issued travel warnings, and the outbreak was expected to significantly impact the tourism industry. Several countries have taken the unusual step of advising their citizens to delay pregnancy until more is known about the virus and its impact on fetal development. With the 2016 Summer Olympics hosted in Rio de Janeiro, health officials worldwide voiced concerns over a potential crisis, both in Brazil and when international athletes and tourists returned home and possibly would spread the virus. Some researchers speculated that only one or two tourists might be infected during the three weeks or approximately 3.2 infections per 100,000 tourists. In November 2016, the World Health Organization declared that the Zika virus was no longer a global emergency while noting that the virus still represents "a highly significant and a long-term problem".

As of August 2017, the number of new Zika virus cases in the Americas had fallen dramatically.

INDIA

On May 15, 2017, three cases of Zika virus infection in India were reported in the state of Gujarat. By late 2018, there had been at least 159 cases in Rajasthan and 127 in Madhya Pradesh.

In July 2021, the first case of Zika virus infection in the Indian state of Kerala was reported. After the first confirmed case, 19 other people who had previously presented symptoms were tested, and 13 of those had positive results, showing that Zika had been circulating in Kerala since at least May 2021. By August 6th, 2021, there had been 65 reported cases in Kerala.

On October 22, 2021, an officer in the Indian Air Force in Kanpur tested positive for the Zika virus, making it the first reported case in the Indian state of Uttar Pradesh.

OTHER CASES

On 22 March 2016, Reuters reported that Zika was isolated from a 2014 blood sample of an elderly man in Chittagong in Bangladesh as part of a retrospective study. Zika is also occurring in Tanzania as of 2016.

Between August and November 2016, 455 cases of Zika virus infection were confirmed in Singapore.

In 2017, Angola reported two cases of Zika fever.

KEY FACTS

Zika virus disease is caused by a virus transmitted primarily by Aedes mosquitoes, which bite during the day.

Symptoms are generally mild and include fever, rash, conjunctivitis, muscle and joint pain, malaise, or headache.

Symptoms typically last for 2–7 days. Most people with Zika virus infection do not develop symptoms.

Zika virus infection during pregnancy can cause infants to be born with microcephaly and other congenital malformations, known as congenital Zika syndrome. Infection with Zika virus is also associated with other complications of pregnancy including preterm birth and miscarriage.

An increased risk of neurologic complications is associated with Zika virus infection in adults and children, including Guillain-Barré syndrome, neuropathy, and myelitis.

ZIKA AND GUILLAIN- BARRE SYNDROME

Guillain-Barré syndrome (GBS) is an uncommon sickness of the nervous system in which a person's immune system damages the nerve cells, causing muscle weakness, and sometimes, paralysis.

Several countries that have experienced Zika outbreaks recently have reported increases in people who have Guillain-Barré syndrome (GBS).

Current CDC research suggests that GBS is strongly associated with Zika; however, only a small proportion of people with recent Zika virus infection get GBS.

GBS symptoms include weakness of the arms and legs and, in severe cases, can affect the muscles that control breathing. These symptoms can last a few weeks or several months. Most people fully recover from GBS, though some people have permanent damage. Very few people die from GBS. Researchers do not fully understand what causes GBS. Most people with GBS report an infection before they have GBS symptoms. Rarely, vaccination has also been associated with the onset of GBS (for example, the 1976 Swine influenza vaccine). An estimated 3,000 to 6,000 people, or 1-2 cases for every 100,000 people, develop GBS each year in the US. Most cases of GBS tend to occur for no known reason, and true "clusters" of cases of GBS are very unusual.

CHAPTER SIX

THE POLIOVIRUS EPIDEMIC

A poliovirus, the causative agent of polio (also known as poliomyelitis), is a serotype of the species Enterovirus C, in the family of Picornaviridae. There are three poliovirus serotypes: types 1, 2, and 3.

Poliovirus is composed of an RNA genome and a protein capsid. The genome is a single-stranded positive-sense RNA (+ssRNA) genome that is about 7500 nucleotides long. The viral particle is about 30 nm in diameter with icosahedral symmetry. Because of its short genome and its simple composition—only RNA and a nonenveloped icosahedral protein coat that encapsulates it, poliovirus is widely regarded as the simplest significant virus.

Poliovirus was first isolated in 1909 by Karl Landsteiner and Erwin Popper. The structure of the virus was first elucidated in 1958 using x-ray diffraction by a team at Birkbeck College led by Rosalind Franklin, showing the poliovirus to have icosahedral symmetry.

In 1981, the poliovirus genome was published by two different teams of researchers: by Vincent Racaniello and David Baltimore at MIT and by Naomi Kitamura and Eckard Wimmer at Stony Brook University.

The three-dimensional structure of poliovirus was determined in 1985 by James Hogle at Scripps Research Institute using X-ray crystallography.

Poliovirus is one of the most well-characterized viruses and has become a useful model system for understanding the biology of RNA viruses.

Poliomyelitis (polio) is a highly infectious viral disease that largely affects children under 5 years of age. The virus is transmitted by person-to-person spread mainly through the fecal-oral route or, less frequently, by a common vehicle (e.g. contaminated water or food) and multiplies in the intestine, from where it can invade the nervous system and cause paralysis.

In 1988, the World Health Assembly adopted a resolution for the worldwide eradication of polio, marking the launch of the Global Polio Eradication Initiative, spearheaded by national governments, WHO, Rotary International, the US Centers for Disease Control and Prevention (CDC), UNICEF, and later joined by the Bill & Melinda Gates Foundation and Gavi, the Vaccine Alliance. Wild poliovirus cases have decreased by over 99% since 1988, from an estimated 350 000 cases in more than 125 endemic countries to 175 reported cases in 2019.

Of the 3 strains of wild poliovirus (type 1, type 2, and type 3), wild poliovirus type 2 was eradicated in 1999 and no case of wild poliovirus type 3 has been found since the last reported case in Nigeria in November 2012. Both strains have officially been certified as globally eradicated. As of 2020, wild poliovirus type 1 affects two countries: Pakistan and Afghanistan.

The strategies for polio eradication work when they are fully implemented. This is demonstrated by India's success in stopping polio in January 2011, in arguably the most technically challenging place, and polio-free certification of the entire WHO Southeast Asia Region in March 2014.

REPLICATION CYCLE

Poliovirus infects human cells by binding to an immunoglobulin-like receptor, CD155 (also known as the poliovirus receptor or

PVR) on the cell surface. Interaction of poliovirus and CD155 facilitates an irreversible conformational change of the viral particle necessary for viral entry. Following attachment to the host cell membrane, entry of the viral nucleic acid was thought to occur one of two ways: via the formation of a pore in the plasma membrane through which the RNA is then "injected" into the host cell cytoplasm, or via virus uptake by receptor-mediated endocytosis. Recent experimental evidence supports the latter hypothesis and suggests that poliovirus binds to CD155 and is taken up by endocytosis. Immediately after the internalization of the particle, the viral RNA is released.

Poliovirus is a positive-stranded RNA virus. Thus, the genome enclosed within the viral particle can be used as messenger RNA and immediately translated by the host cell. On entry, the virus hijacks the cell's translation machinery, causing inhibition of cellular protein synthesis in favor of virus-specific protein production. Unlike the host cell's mRNAs, the 5' end of poliovirus RNA is extremely long—over 700 nucleotides—and highly structured. This region of the viral genome is called an internal ribosome entry site (IRES). This region consists of many secondary structures and 3 or 4 domains. Domain 3 is a self-folding RNA element that contains conserved structural motifs in various stable stem-loops linked by two four-way junctions. As IRES consists of many domains, these domains themselves consist of many loops that contribute to modified translation without a 5' end cap by hijacking ribosomes. The interaction loop of domain 3 is known as GNRA tetraloop. The residues of adenosines A180 and A181 in the GUAA tetraloop form hydrogen bonds via noncanonical base-pairing interactions with the base pairs of the receptors C230/G242 and G231/C241, respectively. Genetic mutations in this region prevent viral protein production. The first IRES to be discovered was found in poliovirus RNA.

Poliovirus mRNA is translated as one long polypeptide. This polypeptide is then autoclaved by internal proteases into about 10 individual viral proteins. Not all cleavages occur with the same efficiency. Therefore, the amounts of proteins produced by the polypeptide cleavage vary: for example, smaller amounts of 3Dpol are produced than those of capsid proteins, VP1–4. These individual viral proteins are:

3Dpol is an RNA-dependent RNA polymerase whose function is to make multiple copies of the viral RNA genome.

2Apro and 3Cpro/3CDpro, proteases that cleave the viral polypeptide.

VPg (3B), is a small protein that binds viral RNA and is necessary for the synthesis of viral positive and negative-strand RNA.

2BC, 2B, 2C (an ATPase)[28], 3AB, 3A, 3B proteins which comprise the protein complex needed for virus replication.

VP0, which is further cleaved into VP2 and VP4, VP1 and VP3, proteins of the viral capsid.

After translation, transcription, and genome replication which involve a single process, synthesis of (+) RNA) is realized. For the infecting (+)RNA to be replicated, multiple copies of (–)RNA must be transcribed and then used as templates for (+)RNA synthesis. Replicative intermediates (RIs), which are an association of RNA molecules consisting of a template RNA and several growing RNAs of varying length, are seen in both the replication complexes for (–)RNAs and (+)RNAs. For the synthesis of each negative-strand and positive-strand RNAs, VPg protein in the poliovirus works as a primer. RNA-dependent RNA polymerase of the poliovirus adds two uracil nucleotides (UU) to VPg protein utilizing the poly(A) tail at the 3′-end of the +ssRNA genome as a pattern for the synthesis of the negative-strand antigenomic RNA. To initiate this –ssRNA synthesis, the tyrosine hydroxyl of VPg is needed. But for the initiation of positive-strand RNA synthesis, CRE-dependent VPg uridylylation is needed. This means that VPg is once more utilized as a primer however this time it adds the two uridine triphosphates using a cis-acting replication element (CRE) as a template.

The CRE of poliovirus is identified as an unachieved base-paired stem and a final loop consisting of 61. The CRE is found in enteroviruses. It is a highly preserved secondary RNA structural element and bedded in the genome's polyprotein-coding region. The complex can be translocated to the 5' region of the genome that has no coding activity, at least 3.7-kb distant from the initial location. This process can occur without negatively influencing activity. CRE copies don't influence replication negatively. Uridylylation process of VPg that takes place at CRE needs the presence of 3CDpro which is an RNA binding protein. It is attached to the CRE directly and specifically. Because of its presence, VPg can bind the CRE properly and primary production proceeds without problems.

Some of the (+) RNA molecules are used as templates for further (–) RNA synthesis, some function as mRNA, and some are destined to be the genomes of progeny virions.

In the assembly of new virus particles (i.e. the packaging of progeny genome into a procapsid which can survive outside the host cell), including, respectively:

Five copies each of VP0, VP3, and VP1 whose N termini and VP4 form interior surface of capsid, assemble into a 'pentamer' and 12 pentamers form a procapsid. (The outer surface of the capsid is consisting of VP1, VP2, VP3; C termini of VP1 and VP3 form the canyons around each of the vertices; around this time, the 60 copies of VP0 are cleaved into VP4 and VP2.)

Each procapsid acquires a copy of the virus genome, with VPg still attached at the 5' end.

Fully assembled poliovirus leaves the confines of its host cell by lysis 4 to 6 hours following initiation of infection in cultured mammalian cells. The mechanism of viral release from the cell is unclear, but each dying cell can release up to 10,000 polio virions.

Drake demonstrated that poliovirus is able can multiplicity reactivation. That is, when polioviruses were irradiated with UV light and allowed to undergo multiple infections of host cells, viable progeny could be formed even at UV doses that inactivated the virus in single infections. Poliovirus can undergo genetic recombination when at least two viral genomes are present in the same host cell. Kirkegaard and Baltimore presented evidence that RNA-dependent RNA polymerase (RdRP) catalyzes recombination by a copy choice mechanism in which the RdRP switches between (+)ssRNA templates during negative-strand synthesis. Recombination in RNA viruses appears to be an adaptive mechanism for repairing genome damage.

POST-POLIO SYNDROME (OPHPR)

Polio has been around since ancient times. This ancient Egyptian tomb painting shows a man with a withered leg unable to bear weight without the use of a walking stick. This means that most muscle fibers are replaced with scarring (muscle-wasting) that is permanent.

If someone had polio as a child or young adult but had kept or recovered some or all movement of weakened arms or legs, even to the point of being athletic afterward, they can risk becoming weaker in late adulthood. That is a post-polio syndrome (PPS), a condition that can affect polio survivors decades after they recover from their initial poliovirus infection. Some PPS patients become wheelchair-bound when they had not been before.

ORIGIN AND SEROTYPES

Poliovirus is structurally similar to other human enteroviruses (coxsackieviruses, echoviruses, and rhinoviruses), which also use immunoglobulin-like molecules to recognize and enter host cells. Phylogenetic analysis of the RNA and protein sequences of poliovirus suggests that it may have evolved from a C-cluster Coxsackie A virus ancestor, that arose through a mutation within the capsid. The distinct speciation of poliovirus probably occurred as a result of a change in cellular receptor specificity from intercellular adhesion molecule-1 (ICAM-1), used by C-cluster

Coxsackie A viruses, to CD155; leading to a change in pathogenicity and allowing the virus to infect nervous tissue.

The mutation rate in the virus is relatively high even for an RNA virus with a synonymous substitution rate of 1.0 x 10−2 substitutions/site/year and a non-synonymous substitution rate of 3.0 x 10−4 substitutions/site/year. Base distribution within the genome is not random with adenosine being less common than expected at the 5’ end and higher at the 3' end. Codon use is not random with codons ending in adenosine being favored and those ending in cytosine or guanine being avoided. Codon use differs between the three genotypes and appears to be driven by mutation rather than selection.

The three serotypes of poliovirus, PV-1, PV-2, and PV-3, each have a slightly different capsid protein. Capsid proteins define cellular receptor specificity and virus antigenicity. PV-1 is the most common form encountered in nature, but all three forms are extremely infectious. As of March 2020, wild PV-1 is highly localized to regions in Pakistan and Afghanistan. Certification of the eradication of indigenous transmission occurred in September 2015 for wild PV-2, after last being detected in 1999, and in October 2019 for wild PV-3, after last being detected in 2012.

Specific strains of each serotype are used to prepare vaccines against polio. Inactive polio vaccine is prepared by formalin inactivation of three wild, virulent reference strains, Mahoney or Brunenders (PV-1), MEF-1/Lansing (PV-2), and Sackett/Leon (PV-3). Oral polio vaccine contains live attenuated (weakened) strains of the three serotypes of poliovirus. Passaging the virus strains in monkey kidney epithelial cells introduces mutations in the viral IRES, and hinders (or attenuates) the ability of the virus to infect nervous tissue.

Polioviruses were formerly classified as a distinct species belonging to the genus Enterovirus in the family Picornaviridae. In 2008, the Poliovirus species was eliminated and the three serotypes were assigned to the species Human enterovirus C (later renamed Enterovirus C), in the genus Enterovirus in the family

Picornaviridae. The type species of the genus Enterovirus was changed from Poliovirus to (Human) Enterovirus C.

Fig. 6.1 Poliovirus

PATHOGENESIS

The primary determinant of infection for any virus is its ability to enter a cell and produce additional infectious particles. The presence of CD155 is thought to define the animals and tissues that can be infected by poliovirus. CD155 is found (outside of laboratories) only on the cells of humans, higher primates, and Old World monkeys. Poliovirus is, however, strictly a human pathogen, and does not naturally infect any other species (although chimpanzees and Old World monkeys can be experimentally infected).

The CD155 gene appears to have been subject to positive selection. The protein has several domains of which domain D1 contains the poliovirus binding site. Within this domain, 37 amino acids are responsible for binding the virus.

Poliovirus is an enterovirus. Infection occurs via the fecal-oral route, meaning that one ingests the virus and viral replication occurs in the alimentary tract The virus is shed in the feces of infected individuals. In 95% of cases, only a primary, transient presence of viremia (virus in the bloodstream) occurs, and the poliovirus infection is asymptomatic. In about 5% of cases, the virus spreads and replicates in other sites such as brown fat, reticuloendothelial tissue, and muscle. The sustained viral replication causes secondary viremia and leads to the development of minor symptoms such as fever, headache, and sore throat. Paralytic poliomyelitis occurs in less than 1% of poliovirus infections. The paralytic disease occurs when the virus enters the central nervous system (CNS) and replicates in motor neurons within the spinal cord, brain stem, or motor cortex, resulting in the selective destruction of motor neurons leading to temporary or permanent paralysis. This is a very rare event in babies, who still have anti-poliovirus antibodies acquired from their mothers. In rare cases, paralytic poliomyelitis leads to respiratory arrest and death. In cases of the paralytic disease, muscle pain and spasms are frequently observed prior tobeforeet of weakness and paralysis. Paralysis typically persists from days to weeks before.

In many respects, the neurological phase of infection is thought to be an accidental diversion of the normal gastrointestinal infection. The mechanisms by which poliovirus enters the CNS are poorly understood. Three non-mutually exclusive hypotheses have been suggested to explain its entry. All theories require primary viremia. The first hypothesis predicts that virions pass directly from the blood into the central nervous system by crossing the blood-brain barrier independent of CD155. A second hypothesis suggests that the virions are transported from peripheral tissues that have been bathed in the viremic blood, for example, muscle tissue, to the spinal cord through nerve pathways via retrograde axonal transport. A third hypothesis is that the virus is imported into the CNS via infected monocytes or macrophages.

Poliomyelitis is a disease of the central nervous system. However, CD155 is believed to be present on the surface of most or all human cells. Therefore, receptor expression does not explain why poliovirus preferentially infects certain tissues. This suggests that tissue tropism is determined after cellular infection. Recent work has suggested that the type I interferon response (specifically that of interferon-alpha and beta) is an important factor that defines which types of cells support poliovirus replication. In mice expressing CD155 (through genetic engineering) but lacking the type I interferon receptor, poliovirus not only replicates in an expanded repertoire of tissue types, but these mice are also able to be infected orally with the virus.

SYMPTOMS

Poliovirus is highly infectious. The incubation period is usually 7–10 days but can range from 4–35 days. The virus enters the body through the mouth and multiplies in the intestine. It then invades the nervous system. Up to 90% of those infected experience no or mild symptoms and the disease usually goes unrecognized. In others, initial symptoms include fever, fatigue, headache, vomiting, stiffness in the neck, and pain in the limbs. These symptoms usually last for 2–10 days and most recovery is complete in almost all cases. However, in the remaining proportion of cases the virus causes paralysis, usually of the legs, which is most often permanent. Paralysis can occur as rapidly as within a few hours of infection. Of those paralyzed, 5-10% die when their breathing muscles become immobilized.

The virus is shed by infected people (usually children) through feces, where it can spread quickly, especially in areas with poor hygiene and sanitation systems. Most people who get infected with poliovirus (about 72 out of 100) will not have any visible symptoms.

About 1 out of 4 people (or 25 out of 100) with poliovirus infection will have flu-like symptoms that may include:

Sore throat, Fever, Tiredness, Nausea, Headache, Stomach pain.

These symptoms usually last 2 to 5 days, then go away on their own. A smaller proportion of people (much less than one out of 100, or 1-5 out of 1000) with poliovirus infection will develop other, more serious symptoms that affect the brain and spinal cord:

Paresthesia (feeling of pins and needles in the legs)

Meningitis (infection of the covering of the spinal cord and/or brain) occurs in about 1 out of 25 people with poliovirus infection.

Paralysis (can't move parts of the body) or weakness in the arms, legs, or both, occurs in about 1 out of 200 people with poliovirus infection.

Paralysis is the most severe symptom associated with polio because it can lead to permanent disability and death. Between 2 and 10 out of 100 people who have paralysis from poliovirus infection die, because the virus affects the muscles that help them breathe. Even children who seem to fully recover can develop new muscle pain, weakness, or paralysis as adults, 15 to 40 years later. This is called post-polio syndrome.

Note that "poliomyelitis" (or "polio" for short) is defined as a paralytic disease. So only people with the paralytic infection are considered to have the disease.

IMMUNE SYSTEM AVOIDANCE

Poliovirus uses two key mechanisms to evade the immune system. First, it is capable of surviving the highly acidic conditions of the stomach, allowing the virus to infect the host and spread throughout the body via the lymphatic system. Second, because it can replicate very quickly, the virus overwhelms the host organs before an immune response can be mounted. If the detail is given at the attachment phase; poliovirus with canyons on the virion surface has virus attachment sites located in pockets at the canyon bases. The canyons are too narrow for access by antibodies, so the virus attachment sites are protected from the host's immune surveillance, while the remainder of the virion surface can mutate to avoid the host's immune response.

Individuals who are exposed to poliovirus, either through infection or by immunization with polio vaccine, develop immunity. In immune individuals, antibodies against poliovirus are present in the tonsils and gastrointestinal tract (specifically IgA antibodies) and are ablecanoliovirus replication; IgG and IgM antibodies against poliovirus can prevent the spread of the virus to motor neurons of the central nervous system. Infection with one serotype of poliovirus does not provide immunity against the other serotypes; however, second attacks within the same individual are extremely rare.

PVR TRANSGENIC MOUSE

Although humans are the only known natural hosts of poliovirus, monkeys can be experimentally infected and they have long been used to study poliovirus. In 1990–91, a small animal model of poliomyelitis was developed by two laboratories. Mice were engineered to express a human receptor to poliovirus (hPVR).

Unlike normal mice, transgenic poliovirus receptor (TgPVR) mice are susceptible to poliovirus injected intravenously or intramuscularly, and when injected directly into the spinal cord or the brain. Upon infection, TgPVR mice show signs of paralysis that resemble those of poliomyelitis in humans and monkeys, and the central nervous systems of paralyzed mice are histocytochemically similar to those of humans and monkeys. This mouse model of human poliovirus infection has proven to be an invaluable tool in understanding poliovirus biology and pathogenicity.

Three distinct types of TgPVR mice have been well studied:

In TgPVR1 mice, the transgene encoding the human PVR was incorporated into mouse chromosome 4. These mice express the highest levels of the transgene and the highest sensitivity to poliovirus. TgPVR1 mice are susceptible to poliovirus through the intraspinal, intracerebral, intramuscular, and intravenous pathways, but not through the oral route.

TgPVR21 mice have incorporated the human PVR at chromosome 13. These mice are less susceptible to poliovirus infection through the intracerebral route, possibly because they express decreased levels of hPVR. TgPVR21 mice have bearable to poliovirus infection through intranasal inoculation and may be useful as a mucosal infection model.

In TgPVR5 mice, the human transgene is located on chromosome 12. These mice exhibit the lowest levels of hPVR expression and are the least susceptible to poliovirus infection.

Recently, a fourth TgPVR mouse model was developed. These "cPVR" mice carry hPVR cDNA, driven by a β-actin promoter, and have proven susceptible to poliovirus through intracerebral, intramuscular, and intranasal routes. In addition, these mice are capable of developing the bulbar form of polio after intranasal inoculation.

The development of the TgPVR mouse has had a profound effect on oral poliovirus vaccine (OPV) production. Previously, monitoring the safety of OPV had to be performed using monkeys, because only primates are susceptible to the virus. In 1999, the World Health Organization approved the use of the TgPVR mouse as an alternative method of assessing the effectiveness of the vaccine against poliovirus type-3. In 2000, the mouse model was approved for tests of vaccines against type-1 and type-2 poliovirus.

CLONING AND SYNTHESIS

In 1981, Racaniello and Baltimore used recombinant DNA technology to generate the first infectious clone of an animal RNA virus, poliovirus. DNA encoding the RNA genome of poliovirus was introduced into cultured mammalian cells and infectious poliovirus was produced. The creation of the infectious clone propelled understanding of poliovirus biology and has become a standard technology used to study many other viruses.

In 2002, Eckard Wimmer's group at Stony Brook University succeeded in synthesizing poliovirus from its chemical code, producing the world's first synthetic virus. Scientists first converted poliovirus's published RNA sequence, 7741 bases long, into a DNA sequence, as DNA was easier to synthesize. Short fragments of this DNA sequence were obtained by mail order and assembled. The complete viral genome was then assembled by a gene synthesis company. Nineteen markers were incorporated into the synthesized DNA so that it could be distinguished from natural poliovirus. Enzymes were used to convert the DNA back into RNA, its natural state. Other enzymes were then used to translate the RNA into a polypeptide, producing functional viral particles. This whole painstaking process took two years. The newly minted synthetic virus was injected into PVR transgenic mice, to determine if the synthetic version was able to cause disease. The synthetic virus was able to replicate, infect, and cause paralysis or death in mice. However, the synthetic version was between 1,000 and 10,000 times weaker than the original virus, probably due to one of the added markers.

TRANSMISSION

Poliovirus is very contagious and spreads through person-to-person contact. It lives in an infected person's throat and intestines. Poliovirus only infects people. It enters the body through the mouth and spreads through:

Contact with the feces (poop) of an infected person.

Droplets from a sneeze or cough of an infected person (less common).

You can get infected with poliovirus if:

You have picked-up minute pieces of feces on your hands, and you touch your mouth.

You put in your mouth objects like toys that are contaminated with feces.

An infected person may spread the virus to others immediately before and up to 2 weeks after symptoms appear.

The virus can live in an infected person's feces for many weeks. It can contaminate food and water in unsanitary conditions.

People who don't have symptoms can still pass the virus to others and make them sick.

EARLY HISTORY

Ancient Egyptian paintings and carvings depict otherwise healthy people with withered limbs, and children walking with canes at a young age. It is theorized that the Roman Emperor Claudius was stricken as a child, and this caused him to walk with a limp for the rest of his life. Perhaps the earliest recorded case of poliomyelitis is that of Sir Walter Scott. In 1773, Scott was said to have developed "a severe teething fever which deprived him of the power of his right leg". At the time, polio was not known to medicine. A retrospective diagnosis of polio is considered to be strong due to the detailed account Scott later made, and the resultant lameness of his right leg had an important effect on his life and writing.

The symptoms of poliomyelitis have been described by many names. In the early nineteenth century, the disease was known variously as Dental Paralysis, Infantile Spinal Paralysis, Essential Paralysis of Children, Regressive Paralysis, Myelitis of the Anterior Horns, Tephromyelitis (from the Greek tephros, meaning "ash-gray"), and Paralysis of the Morning. In 1789 the first clinical description of poliomyelitis was provided by the British physician Michael Underwood—he refers to polio as "a debility of the lower extremities". The first medical report on poliomyelitis was by Jakob Heine, in 1840; he called the disease Lähmungszustände der unteren Extremitäten ("Paralysis of the Lower Extremities"). Karl Oskar Medin was the first to empirically study a poliomyelitis epidemic in 1890.[13] This work, and the prior classification by Heine, led to the disease being known as Heine-Medin disease.

EPIDEMICS

Major polio epidemics were unknown before the 20th century; localized paralytic polio epidemics began to appear in Europe and the United States around 1900. The first report of multiple polio cases was published in 1843 and described an 1841 outbreak in Louisiana. A fifty-year gap occurs before the next U.S. report—a cluster of 26 cases in Boston in 1893. The first recognized U.S. polio epidemic occurred the following year in Vermont with 132 total cases (18 deaths), including several cases in adults. Numerous epidemics of varying magnitude began to appear throughout the country; by 1907 approximately 2,500 cases of poliomyelitis were reported in New York City.

On Saturday, June 17, 1916, an official announcement of the existence of an epidemic polio infection was made in Brooklyn, New York. That year, there were over 27,000 cases and more than 6,000 deaths due to polio in the United States, with over 2,000 deaths in New York City alone. The names and addresses of individuals with confirmed polio cases were published daily in the press, their houses were identified with placards, and their families were quarantined. Dr. Hiram M. Hiller, Jr. was one of the physicians in several cities who realized what they were dealing with, but the nature of the disease remained largely a mystery. The 1916 epidemic caused widespread panic and thousands fled the city to nearby mountain resorts; movie theaters were closed, meetings were canceled, public gatherings were almost nonexistent, and children were warned not to drink from water fountains, and told to avoid amusement parks, swimming pools, and beaches. From 1916 onward, a polio epidemic appeared each summer in at least one part of the country, with the most serious occurring in the 1940s and 1950s. In the epidemic of 1949, 42,173 cases were reported in the United States and 2,720 deaths from the disease occurred. Canada and the United Kingdom were also affected.

Before the century, polio infections were rarely seen in infants before 6 months of age, and most cases occurred in children 6 months to 4 years of age. Young children who contract polio generally suffer only mild symptoms, but as a result, they become permanently immune to the disease. In developed countries during the late 19th and early 20th centuries, improvements were being made in community sanitation, including improved sewage disposal and clean water supplies. Better hygiene meant that infants and young children had fewer opportunities to encounter and develop immunity to polio. Exposure to poliovirus was therefore delayed until late childhood or adult life when it was more likely to take the paralytic form.

In children, paralysis due to polio occurs in one in 1000 cases, while in adults, paralysis occurs in one in 75 cases. By 1950, the peak age incidence of paralytic poliomyelitis in the United States had shifted from infants to children aged 5 to 9 years; about one-third of the cases were reported in persons over 15 years of age. Accordingly, the rate of paralysis and death due to polio infection also increased during this time. In the United States, the 1952 polio epidemic was the worst outbreak in the nation's history and is credited with heightening parents' fears of the disease and focusing public awareness on the need for a vaccine. Of the 57,628 cases reported that year, 3,145 died and 21,269 were left with mild to disabling paralysis.

ANTERIOR POLIOMYELITIS!

INFANTILE PARALYSIS

"Act of Assembly approved May 14, 1909, provides that anyone violating the provisions of this Act, upon conviction thereof may be sentenced to pay a fine of not less than $10.00 or more than $100.00, to be paid to the use of said county, or to be imprisoned in the county jail for a period of not less than ten days or more than thirty days, or both, at the discretion of the court."

BY ORDER OF THE BOARD OF HEALTH.

Health Officer.

Address.

Fig. 6.2 Cardboard Polio Placard

HISTORICAL TREATMENTS

In the early 20th century—in the absence of proven treatments—a number several potentially dangerous polio treatments were suggested. In John Haven Emerson's A Monograph on the Epidemic of Poliomyelitis (Infantile Paralysis) in New York City in 1916 one suggested remedy reads:

Give oxygen through the lower extremities, by positive electricity. Frequent baths using almond meal, or oxidizing the water. Applications of poultices of Roman chamomile, slippery elm, arnica, mustard, cantharis, amygdalae Dulcis oil, and of special merit, spikenard oil and Xanthoxolinum. Internally use caffeine, Fl. Kola, dry muriate of quinine, the elixir of cinchona, radium water, chloride of gold, liquor calcis, and wine of pepsin.

Following the 1916 epidemics and having experienced little success in treating polio patients, researchers set out to find new and better treatments for the disease. Between 1917 and the early 1950s, several therapies were explored to prevent deformities, including hydrotherapy and electrotherapy.

In 1939, Albert Sabin reported that "In the experiments reported in the present communication it was found that vitamin C, both natural and synthetic preparations, did not affect the course of experimental poliomyelitis induced by nasal instillation of the virus."

Surgical treatments such as nerve grafting, tendon lengthening, tendon transfers, and limb lengthening and shortening were used extensively during this time. Patients with residual paralysis were treated with braces and taught to compensate for lost function with the help of calipers, crutches, and wheelchairs. The use of devices such as rigid braces and body casts, which tended to cause muscle atrophy due to the limited movement of the user, was also touted as effective treatments. Massage and passive motion exercises were also used to treat polio victims. Most of these treatments proved to be of little therapeutic value, however several effective support measures for the treatment of polio did emerge during these decades including the iron lung, an anti-polio antibody serum, and a treatment regimen developed by Sister Elizabeth Kenny.

IRON LUNG

The first iron lung used in the treatment of polio victims was invented by Philip Drinker, Louis Agassiz Shaw, and James Wilson at Harvard, and tested October 12, 1928, at Children's Hospital, Boston. The original Drinker iron lung was powered by an electric motor attached to two vacuum cleaners and worked by changing the pressure inside the machine. When the pressure is lowered, the chest cavity expands, trying to fill this partial vacuum. When the pressure is raised the chest cavity contracts. This expansion and contraction mimic the physiology of normal breathing. The design of the iron lung was subsequently improved by using a bellows attached directly to the machine, and John Haven Emerson modified the design to make production less expensive. The Emerson Iron Lung was produced until 1970. Other respiratory aids were used, such as the Bragg-Paul Pulsator and the "rocking bed" for patients with less critical breathing difficulties.

During the polio epidemics, the iron lung saved many thousands of lives, but the machine was large, cumbersome, and very expensive: in the 1930s, an iron lung cost about $1,500—about the same price as the average home. The cost of running the machine was also prohibitive, as patients were encased in the metal chambers for months, years, and sometimes for life. Even with an iron lung, the fatality rate for patients with bulbar polio exceeded 90%.

These drawbacks led to the development of more modern positive-pressure ventilators and the use of positive-pressure ventilation by tracheostomy. Positive pressure ventilators reduced mortality in bulbar patients from 90% to 20%. In the Copenhagen epidemic of 1952, large numbers of patients were ventilated by hand ("bagged") by medical students and anyone else on hand because of the large number of bulbar polio patients and the small number of ventilators available.

Fig. 6.3 An Iron Lung

PASSIVE IMMUNOTHERAPY

In 1950 William Hammon at the University of Pittsburgh isolated serum, containing antibodies against poliovirus, from the blood of polio survivors. The serum, Hammon believed, would prevent the spread of polio and reduce the severity of disease in polio patients. Between September 1951 and July 1952 nearly 55,000 children were involved in a clinical trial of the anti-polio serum. The results of the trial were promising; the serum was shown to be about 80% effective in preventing the development of paralytic poliomyelitis, and protection was shown to last for 5 weeks if given under tightly controlled circumstances. The serum was also shown to reduce the severity of the disease in patients who developed polio.

The antibody serum was widely administered, but obtaining the serum was an expensive and time-consuming process, and the focus of the medical community soon shifted to the development of a polio vaccine.

KENNY REGIMEN

Early management practices for paralyzed muscles emphasized the need to rest the affected muscles and suggested that the application of splints would prevent tightening of muscle, tendons, ligaments, or skin that would prevent normal movement. Many paralyzed polio patients lay in plaster body casts for months at a time. This prolonged casting often resulted in atrophy of both affected and unaffected muscles.

In 1940, Sister Elizabeth Kenny, an Australian bush nurse from Queensland, arrived in North America and challenged this approach to treatment. In treating polio cases in rural Australia between 1928 and 1940, Kenny had developed a form of physical therapy that—instead of immobilizing afflicted limbs—aimed to relieve pain and spasms in polio patients through the use of hot, moist packs to relieve muscle spasms and early activity and exercise to maximize the strength of unaffected muscle fibers and promote the neuroplastic recruitment of remaining nerve cells that had not been killed by the virus. Sister Kenny later settled in Minnesota where she established the Sister Kenny Rehabilitation Institute, beginning a worldwide crusade to advocate her system of treatment. Slowly, Kenny's ideas won acceptance, and by the mid-20th century had become the hallmark for the treatment of paralytic polio. In combination with antispasmodic medications to reduce muscular contractions, Kenny's therapy is still used in the treatment of paralytic poliomyelitis.

In 2009 as part of the Q150 celebrations, the Kenny regimen for polio treatment was announced as one of the Q150 Icons of Queensland for its role as an iconic "innovation and invention".

VACCINE DEVELOPMENT

In 1935 Maurice Brodie, a research assistant at New York University and William Hallock Park of the New York City Department of Health, attempted to produce a polio vaccine, procured from the virus in ground-up monkey spinal cords, and killed by formaldehyde. Brodie first tested the vaccine on himself and several of his assistants. He then gave the vaccine to three thousand children. Many developed allergic reactions, but none of the children developed an immunity to polio. During the late 1940s and early 1950s, a research group, headed by John Enders at the Boston Children's Hospital, successfully cultivated the poliovirus in human tissue. This significant breakthrough ultimately allowed for the development of polio vaccines. Enders and his colleagues, Thomas H. Weller and Frederick C. Robbins, were recognized for their labors with the Nobel Prize in 1954.

Two vaccines are used throughout the world to combat polio. The first was developed by Jonas Salk, first tested in 1952 using the HeLa cell, and announced to the world by Salk on April 12, 1955. The Salk vaccine, or inactivated poliovirus vaccine (IPV), consists of an injected dose of killed poliovirus. In 1954, the vaccine was tested for its ability to prevent polio; its field trials grew to be the largest medical experiment in history. In 1955, it was chosen for use throughout the United States. By 1957, following mass immunizations promoted by the March of Dimes, the annual number of polio cases in the United States was reduced, from a peak of nearly 58,000 cases to 5,600 cases.

Eight years after Salk's success, Albert Sabin developed an oral polio vaccine (OPV) using a live but weakened (attenuated) virus. Human trials of Sabin's vaccine began in 1957 and it was licensed in 1962. Following the development of the oral polio vaccine, the second wave of mass immunizations led to a further decline in the number of cases: by 1961, only 161 cases were recorded in the United States.[50] The last cases of paralytic poliomyelitis caused by the endemic transmission of poliovirus in the United States were in 1979 when an outbreak occurred among the Amish in several Midwestern states.

DISABILITY RIGHTS MOVEMENT

As thousands of polio survivors with varying degrees of paralysis left the rehabilitation hospitals and went home, to school, and work, many were frustrated by the lack of accessibility and discrimination they experienced in their communities. In the early twentieth century, the use of a wheelchair at home or out in public was a daunting prospect as no public transportation system accommodated wheelchairs, and most public buildings including schools were inaccessible to those with disabilities. Many children left disabled by polio were forced to attend separate institutions for "crippled children" or had to be carried up and downstairs.

As people who had been paralyzed by polio matured, they began to demand the right to participate in the mainstream of society. Polio survivors were often at the forefront of the disability rights movement that emerged in the United States during the 1970s and pushed legislation such as the Rehabilitation Act of 1973 which protected qualified individuals from discrimination based on their disability, and the Americans with Disabilities Act of 1990. Other political movements led by polio survivors include the Independent Living and Universal design movements of the 1960s and 1970s.

Polio survivors are one of the largest disabled groups in the world. The World Health Organization estimates that there are 10 to 20 million polio survivors worldwide. In 1977, the National Health Interview Survey reported that 254,000 people were living in the United States who had been paralyzed by polio. According to local polio support groups and doctors, some 40,000 polio survivors with varying degrees of paralysis live in Germany, 30,000 in Japan,

24,000 in France, 16,000 in Australia, 12,000 in Canada, and 12,000 in the United Kingdom.

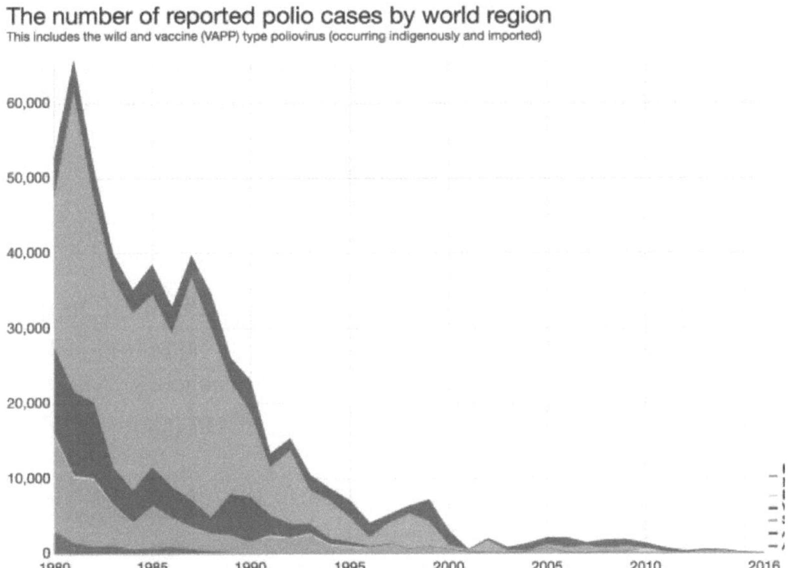

Fig. 6.4 Number of Polio Cases

CHAPTER SEVEN

THE YELLOW FEVER

Yellow fever is a viral disease of typically short duration. In most cases, symptoms include fever, chills, loss of appetite, nausea, muscle pains – particularly in the back – and headaches. Symptoms typically improve within five days. In about 15% of people, within a day of improving the fever comes back, abdominal pain occurs, and liver damage begins causing yellow skin. If this occurs, the risk of bleeding and kidney problems is increased.

The yellow fever virus is found in tropical and subtropical areas of Africa and South America. The virus is spread to people by the bite of an infected mosquito. Yellow fever is a very rare cause of illness in U.S. travelers. Illness ranges from a fever with aches and pains to severe liver disease with bleeding and yellowing skin (jaundice). Yellow fever infection is diagnosed based on laboratory testing, a person's symptoms, and travel history. There is no medicine to treat or cure the infection. To prevent getting sick from yellow fever, use insect repellent, wear long-sleeved shirts and long pants, and get vaccinated.

The disease is caused by the yellow fever virus and is spread by the bite of an infected mosquito. It infects only humans, other primates, and several types of mosquitoes. In cities, it is spread primarily by Aedes aegypti, a type of mosquito found throughout the tropics and subtropics. The virus is an RNA virus of the genus Flavivirus. The disease may be difficult to tell apart from other illnesses, especially in the early stages. To confirm a suspected case, blood sample testing with polymerase chain reaction is required.

A safe and effective vaccine against yellow fever exists, and some countries require vaccinations for travelers. Other efforts to prevent infection include reducing the population of transmitting mosquitoes. In areas where yellow fever is common, early diagnosis of cases and immunization of large parts of the population are important to prevent outbreaks. Once a person is infected, management is symptomatic; no specific measures are effective against the virus. Death occurs in up to half of those who get the severe disease.

In 2013, yellow fever resulted in about 127,050 severe infections and 45,000 deaths worldwide, with nearly 90 percent of these occurring in Africa. Nearly a billion people live in an area of the world where the disease is common. It is common in tropical areas of the continents of South America and Africa, but not in Asia. Since the 1980s, the number of cases of yellow fever has been increasing. This is believed to be due to fewer people being immune, more people living in cities, people moving frequently, and changing climate increasing the habitat for mosquitoes.

The disease originated in Africa and spread to the American Continent starting in the 15th century with the European trafficking of enslaved Africans from sub-Saharan Africa. Since the 17th century, several major outbreaks of the disease have occurred in the Americas, Africa, and Europe. In the 18th and 19th centuries, yellow fever was considered one of the most dangerous infectious diseases; numerous epidemics swept through major cities of the US and in other parts of the world.

In 1927, the yellow fever virus was the first human virus to be isolated.

SIGNS AND SYMPTOMS

Yellow fever begins after an incubation period of three to six days. Most cases cause only a mild infection with fever, headache, chills, back pain, fatigue, loss of appetite, muscle pain, nausea, and vomiting. In these cases, the infection lasts only three to six days.

Once contracted, the yellow fever virus incubates in the body for 3 to 6 days. Many people do not experience symptoms, but when these do occur, the most common are fever, muscle pain with prominent backache, headache, loss of appetite, and nausea or vomiting. In most cases, symptoms disappear after 3 to 4 days.

A small percentage of patients, however, enter a second, more toxic phase within 24 hours of recovering from initial symptoms. High fever returns and several body systems are affected, usually the liver and the kidneys. In this phase, people are likely to develop jaundice (yellowing of the skin and eyes, hence the name 'yellow fever'), dark urine, and abdominal pain with vomiting. Bleeding can occur from the mouth, nose, eyes, or stomach. Half of the patients who enter the toxic phase die within 7 - 10 days.

But in 15% of cases, people enter a second, toxic phase of the disease characterized by recurring fever, this time accompanied by jaundice due to liver damage, as well as abdominal pain. Bleeding in the mouth, nose, eyes, and gastrointestinal tract cause vomit containing blood, hence the Spanish name for yellow fever, vómito negro ("black vomit"). There may also be kidney failure, hiccups, and delirium.

Among those who develop jaundice, the fatality rate is 20 to 50%, while the overall fatality rate is about 3 to 7.5%. Severe cases may have mortality greater than 50%.

Surviving the infection provides lifelong immunity, and normally results in no permanent organ damage.

Most people will not have symptoms.

Some people will develop yellow fever illness with initial symptoms including:

Sudden onset of fever, Chills, Severe headache, Back pain, General body aches, Nausea, Vomiting, Fatigue (feeling tired), Weakness.

Most people with the initial symptoms improve within one week.

For some people who recover, weakness and fatigue (feeling tired) might last several months.

A few people will develop a more severe form of the disease. For 1 out of 7 people who have the initial symptoms, there will be a brief remission (a time you feel better) that may last only a few hours or for a day, followed by a more severe form of the disease.

Severe symptoms include:

High fever, Yellow skin (jaundice), Bleeding, Shock, Organ failure.

Severe yellow fever disease can be deadly. If you develop any of these symptoms, see a healthcare provider immediately. Among those who develop severe disease, 30-60% die.

CAUSE

Yellow fever is caused by the yellow fever virus, an enveloped RNA virus 40–50 nm in width, the type species and namesake of the family Flaviviridae. It was the first illness shown to be transmissible by filtered human serum and transmitted by mosquitoes, by American doctor Walter Reed around 1900. The positive-sense, single-stranded RNA is around 10,862 nucleotides long and has a single open reading frame encoding a polyprotein. Host proteases cut this polyprotein into three structural (C, prM, E) and seven nonstructural proteins (NS1, NS2A, NS2B, NS3, NS4A, NS4B, NS5); the enumeration corresponds to the arrangement of the protein-coding genes in the genome. Minimal yellow fever virus (YFV) 3‘UTR region is required for stalling of the host 5’-3' exonuclease XRN1. The UTR contains a PKS3 pseudoknot structure, which serves as a molecular signal to stall the exonuclease and is the only viral requirement for subgenomic flavivirus RNA (sfRNA) production. The sfRNAs are a result of incomplete degradation of the viral genome by the exonuclease and are important for viral pathogenicity. Yellow fever belongs to the group of hemorrhagic fevers.

The viruses infect, amongst others, monocytes, macrophages, Schwann cells, and dendritic cells. They attach to the cell surfaces via specific receptors and are taken up by an endosomal vesicle. Inside the endosome, the decreased pH induces the fusion of the endosomal membrane with the virus envelope. The capsid enters the cytosol, decays, and releases the genome. Receptor binding, as well as membrane fusion, are catalyzed by the protein E, which changes its conformation at low pH, causing a rearrangement of the 90 homodimers to 60 homotrimers.

After entering the host cell, the viral genome is replicated in the rough endoplasmic reticulum (ER) and the so-called vesicle packets. At first, an immature form of the virus particle is produced inside the ER, whose M-protein is not yet cleaved to its mature form, so is denoted as precursor M (prM) and forms a complex with protein E. The immature particles are processed in the Golgi apparatus by the host protein furin, which cleaves prM to M. This releases E from the complex, which can now take its place in the mature, infectious virion.

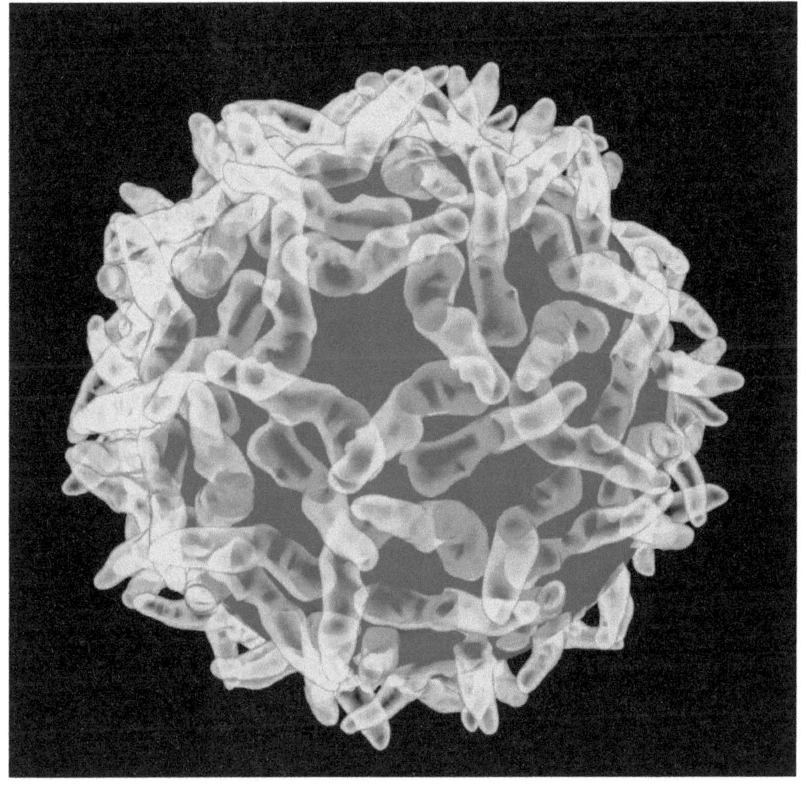

Fig. 7.1 Yellow Fever Virus

TRANSMISSION

Yellow fever virus is mainly transmitted through the bite of the yellow fever mosquito Aedes aegypti, but other mostly Aedes mosquitoes such as the tiger mosquito (Aedes albopictus) can also serve as a vector for this virus. Like other arboviruses, which are transmitted by mosquitoes, the yellow fever virus is taken up by a female mosquito when it ingests the blood of an infected human or another primate. Viruses reach the stomach of the mosquito, and if the virus concentration is high enough, the virions can infect epithelial cells and replicate there. From there, they reach the hemocoel (the blood system of mosquitoes) and from there the salivary glands. When the mosquito next sucks blood, it injects its saliva into the wound, and the virus reaches the bloodstream of the bitten person. Transovarial and transstadial transmission of yellow fever virus within A. aegypti, that is, the transmission from a female mosquito to her eggs and then larvae, are indicated. This infection of vectors without a previous blood meal seems to play a role in single, sudden breakouts of the disease.

Three epidemiologically different infectious cycles occur in which the virus is transmitted from mosquitoes to humans or other primates. In the "urban cycle", only the yellow fever mosquito A. aegypti is involved. It is well adapted to urban areas, and can also transmit other diseases, including Zika fever, dengue fever, and chikungunya. The urban cycle is responsible for the major outbreaks of yellow fever that occur in Africa. Except for an outbreak in Bolivia in 1999, this urban cycle no longer exists in South America.

Besides the urban cycle, both in Africa and South America, a sylvatic cycle (forest or jungle cycle) is present, where Aedes africanus (in Africa) or mosquitoes of the genus Haemagogus and Sabethes (in South America) serve as vectors. In the jungle, the mosquitoes infect mainly nonhuman primates; the disease is mostly asymptomatic in African primates. In South America, the sylvatic cycle is currently the only way humans can become infected, which explains the low incidence of yellow fever cases on the continent. People who become infected in the jungle can carry the virus to urban areas, where A. aegypti acts as a vector. Because of this sylvatic cycle, yellow fever cannot be eradicated except by eradicating the mosquitoes that serve as vectors.

In Africa, a third infectious cycle is known as the "savannah cycle" or intermediate cycle occurs between the jungle and urban cycles. Different mosquitoes of the genus Aedes are involved. In recent years, this has been the most common form of transmission of yellow fever in Africa. Concern exists about yellow fever spreading to Southeast Asia, where its vector A. aegypti already occurs.

The yellow fever virus is an arbovirus of the flavivirus genus and is transmitted by mosquitoes, belonging to the Aedes and Haemogogus species. The different mosquito species live in different habitats - some breed around houses (domestic), others in the jungle (wild), and some in both habitats (semi-domestic). There are 3 types of transmission cycles:

Sylvatic (or jungle) yellow fever: In tropical rainforests, monkeys, which are the primary reservoir of yellow fever, are bitten by wild mosquitoes of the Aedes and Haemogogus species, which pass the virus on to other monkeys. Occasionally humans working or traveling in the forest are bitten by infected mosquitoes and develop yellow fever.

Intermediate yellow fever: In this type of transmission, semi-domestic mosquitoes (those that breed both in the wild and around households) infect both monkeys and people. Increased contact between people and infected mosquitoes leads to increased transmission and many separate villages in an area can develop outbreaks at the same time. This is the most common type of outbreak in Africa.

Urban yellow fever: Large epidemics occur when infected people introduce the virus into heavily populated areas with a high density of Aedes aegypti mosquitoes and where most people have little or no immunity, due to lack of vaccination or prior exposure to yellow fever. In these conditions, infected mosquitoes transmit the virus from person to person.

PATHOGENESIS

After transmission from a mosquito, the viruses replicate in the lymph nodes and infect dendritic cells in particular. From there, they reach the liver and infect hepatocytes (probably indirectly via Kupffer cells), which leads to eosinophilic degradation of these cells and the release of cytokines. Apoptotic masses known as Councilman bodies appear in the cytoplasm of hepatocytes.

Fatality may occur when cytokine storm, shock, and multiple organ failure follow.

DIAGNOSIS

Yellow fever is most frequently a clinical diagnosis, based on symptomatology and travel history. Mild cases of the disease can only be confirmed virologically. Since mild cases of yellow fever can also contribute significantly to regional outbreaks, every suspected case of yellow fever (involving symptoms of fever, pain, nausea, and vomiting 6–10 days after leaving the affected area) is treated seriously.

If yellow fever is suspected, the virus cannot be confirmed until 6–10 days following the illness. A direct confirmation can be obtained by reverse transcription-polymerase chain reaction, where the genome of the virus is amplified. Another direct approach is the isolation of the virus and its growth in cell culture using blood plasma; this can take 1–4 weeks.

Serologically, an enzyme-linked immunosorbent assay during the acute phase of the disease using specific IgM against yellow fever or an increase in specific IgG titer (compared to an earlier sample) can confirm yellow fever. Together with clinical symptoms, the detection of IgM or a four-fold increase in IgG titer is considered a sufficient indication for yellow fever. As these tests can cross-react with other flaviviruses, such as the dengue virus, these indirect methods cannot conclusively prove yellow fever infection.

Liver biopsy can verify inflammation and necrosis of hepatocytes and detect viral antigens. Because of the bleeding tendency of yellow fever patients, a biopsy is only advisable post mortem to confirm the cause of death.

In a differential diagnosis, infections with yellow fever must be distinguished from other feverish illnesses such as malaria. Other viral hemorrhagic fevers, such as Ebola virus, Lassa virus, Marburg virus, and Junin virus, must be excluded as the cause.

Yellow fever is difficult to diagnose, especially during the early stages. A more severe case can be confused with severe malaria, leptospirosis, viral hepatitis (especially fulminant forms), other hemorrhagic fevers, infection with other flaviviruses (such as dengue hemorrhagic fever), and poisoning.

Polymerase chain reaction (PCR) testing in blood and urine can sometimes detect the virus in the early stages of the disease. In later stages, testing to identify antibodies is needed (ELISA and PRNT).

PREVENTION

Personal prevention of yellow fever includes vaccination and avoidance of mosquito bites in areas where yellow fever is endemic. Institutional measures for the prevention of yellow fever include vaccination programs and measures to control mosquitoes. Programs for the distribution of mosquito nets for use in homes produce reductions in cases of both malaria and yellow fever. Use of EPA-registered insect repellent is recommended when outdoors. Exposure for even a short time is enough for a potential mosquito bite. Long-sleeved clothing, long pants, and socks are useful for prevention. The application of larvicides to water-storage containers can help eliminate potential mosquito breeding sites. EPA-registered insecticide spray decreases the transmission of yellow fever.

Use insect repellent when outdoors such as those containing DEET, picaridin, ethyl butylacetylaminopropionate (IR3535), or oil of lemon eucalyptus on exposed skin.

Wear proper clothing to reduce mosquito bites. When weather permits, wear long sleeves, long pants, and socks when outdoors. Mosquitoes may bite through thin clothing, so spraying clothes with repellent containing permethrin or another EPA-registered repellent gives extra protection. Clothing treated with permethrin is commercially available. Mosquito repellents containing permethrin are not approved for application directly to the skin.

The peak biting times for many mosquito species are dusk to dawn. However, A. aegypti, one of the mosquitoes that transmit the yellow fever virus, feeds during the daytime. Staying in accommodations with screened or air-conditioned rooms, particularly during peak biting times, also reduces the risk of mosquito bites.

VACCINATION

Vaccination is recommended for those traveling to affected areas because non-native people tend to develop more severe illnesses when infected. Protection begins on the 10th day after vaccine administration in 95% of people and had been reported to last for at least 10 years. The World Health Organization (WHO) now states that a single dose of vaccine is sufficient to confer lifelong immunity against yellow fever disease. The attenuated live vaccine stem 17D was developed in 1937 by Max Theiler. The WHO recommends routine vaccination for people living in affected areas between the 9th and 12th months after birth.

Vaccination is the most important means of preventing yellow fever. The yellow fever vaccine is safe, affordable and a single dose provides life-long protection against yellow fever disease. A booster dose of the yellow fever vaccine is not needed.

Several vaccination strategies are used to prevent yellow fever disease and transmission: routine infant immunization; mass vaccination campaigns designed to increase coverage in countries at risk; and vaccination of travelers going to yellow fever endemic areas. In high-risk areas where vaccination coverage is low, prompt recognition and control of outbreaks using mass immunization are critical. It is important to vaccinate most (80% or more) of the population at risk to prevent transmission in a region with a yellow fever outbreak.

There have been rare reports of serious side effects from the yellow fever vaccine. The rates for these severe 'adverse events following immunization' (AEFI), when the vaccine provokes an attack on the liver, the kidneys, or on the nervous system are between 0 and 0.21 cases per 10 000 doses in regions where yellow fever is endemic, and from 0.09 to 0.4 cases per 10 000 doses in populations not exposed to the virus.

The risk of AEFI is higher for people over 60 years of age and anyone with severe immunodeficiency due to symptomatic HIV/AIDS or other causes, or who have a thymus disorder. People over 60 years of age should be given the vaccine after a careful risk-benefit assessment.

People who are usually excluded from vaccination include:

Infants aged less than 9 months, people with severe allergies to egg protein, people with severe immunodeficiency due to symptomatic HIV/AIDS or other causes, or who have a thymus disorder.

In accordance with the International Health Regulations (IHR), countries have the right to require travelers to provide a certificate of yellow fever vaccination. If there are medical grounds for not getting vaccinated, this must be certified by the appropriate authorities. The IHR is a legally binding framework to stop the spread of infectious diseases and other health threats. Requiring the certificate of vaccination from travelers is at the discretion of each State Party, and it is not currently required by all countries.

Up to one in four people experience fever, aches, and local soreness and redness at the site of injection. In rare cases (less than one in 200,000 to 300,000), the vaccination can cause yellow fever vaccine-associated viscerotropic disease, which is fatal in 60% of cases. It is probably due to the genetic morphology of the immune system. Another possible side effect is an infection of the nervous system, which occurs in one in 200,000 to 300,000 cases, causing yellow fever vaccine-associated neurotropic disease, which can lead to meningoencephalitis and is fatal in less than 5% of cases.

The Yellow Fever Initiative, launched by the WHO in 2006, vaccinated more than 105 million people in 14 countries in West Africa. No outbreaks were reported during 2015. The campaign was supported by the GAVI alliance and governmental organizations in Europe and Africa. According to the WHO, mass vaccination cannot eliminate yellow fever because of the vast number of infected mosquitoes in urban areas of the target countries, but it will significantly reduce the number of people infected.

Demand for yellow fever vaccines has continued to increase due to the growing number of countries implementing yellow fever vaccination as part of their routine immunization programs. Recent upsurges in yellow fever outbreaks in Angola (2015), the Democratic Republic of Congo (2016), Uganda (2016), and more recently in Nigeria and Brazil in 2017 have further increased demand while straining global vaccine supply. Therefore, to vaccinate susceptible populations in preventive mass immunization campaigns during outbreaks, fractional dosing of the vaccine is being considered as a dose-sparing strategy to maximize limited vaccine supplies. Fractional dose yellow fever vaccination refers to the administration of a reduced volume of vaccine dose, which has been reconstituted as per manufacturer recommendations. The first practical use of fractional dose yellow fever vaccination was in response to a large yellow fever outbreak in the Democratic Republic of the Congo in mid-2016.

In March 2017, the WHO launched a vaccination campaign in Brazil with 3.5 million doses from an emergency stockpile. In March 2017 the WHO recommended vaccination for travelers to certain parts of Brazil. In March 2018, Brazil shifted its policy and announced it planned to vaccinate all 77.5 million currently unvaccinated citizens by April 2019.

COMPULSORY VACCINATION

Some countries in Asia are considered to be potentially in danger of yellow fever epidemics, as both mosquitoes with the capability to transmit yellow fever as well as susceptible monkeys are present. The disease does not yet occur in Asia. To prevent the introduction of the virus, some countries demand previous vaccination of foreign visitors who have passed through yellow fever areas. Vaccination has to be proved by a vaccination certificate, which is valid 10 days after the vaccination and lasts for 10 years. Although the WHO on 17 May 2013 advised that subsequent booster vaccinations are unnecessary, an older (than 10 years) certificate may not be acceptable at all border posts in all affected countries. A list of the countries that require yellow fever vaccination is published by the WHO. If the vaccination cannot be given for some reason, dispensation may be possible. In this case, an exemption certificate issued by a WHO-approved vaccination center is required. Although 32 of 44 countries where yellow fever occurs endemically do have vaccination programs, in many of these countries, less than 50% of their population is vaccinated.

VECTOR CONTROL

Control of the yellow fever mosquito A. aegypti is of major importance, especially because the same mosquito can also transmit dengue fever and chikungunya disease. A. aegypti breeds preferentially in water, for example, in installations by inhabitants of areas with precarious drinking water supplies, or in domestic refuse, especially tires, cans, and plastic bottles. These conditions are common in urban areas in developing countries.

Two main strategies are employed to reduce A. aegypti populations. One approach is to kill the developing larvae. Measures are taken to reduce the water accumulations in which the larvae develop. Larvicides are used, along with larvae-eating fish and copepods, which reduce the number of larvae. For many years, copepods of the genus Mesocyclops have been used in Vietnam for preventing dengue fever. This eradicated the mosquito vector in several areas. Similar efforts may prove effective against yellow fever. Pyriproxyfen is recommended as a chemical larvicide, mainly because it is safe for humans and effective in small doses.

The second strategy is to reduce the population of the adult yellow fever mosquito. Lethal ovitraps can reduce Aedes populations, using lesser amounts of pesticide because it targets the pest directly. Curtains and lids of water tanks can be sprayed with insecticides, but application inside houses is not recommended by the WHO. Insecticide-treated mosquito nets are effective, just as they are against the Anopheles mosquito that carries malaria.

The risk of yellow fever transmission in urban areas can be reduced by eliminating potential mosquito breeding sites, including by applying larvicides to water storage containers and other places where standing water collects. Both vector surveillance and control are components of the prevention and control of vector-borne diseases, especially for transmission control in epidemic situations. For yellow fever, vector surveillance targeting Aedes aegypti and other Aedes species will help inform where there is a risk of an urban outbreak.

Understanding the distribution of these mosquitoes within a country can allow a country to prioritize areas to strengthen their human disease surveillance and testing, and to consider vector control activities. There is currently a limited public health arsenal of safe, efficient, and cost-effective insecticides that can be used against adult vectors. This is mainly due to the resistance of major vectors to common insecticides and the withdrawal or abandonment of certain pesticides for reasons of safety or the high cost of re-registration.

Historically, mosquito control campaigns successfully eliminated Aedes aegypti, the urban yellow fever vector, from most of Central and South America. However, Aedes aegypti has re-colonized urban areas in the region, raising a renewed risk of urban yellow fever. Mosquito control programs targeting wild mosquitoes in forested areas are not practical for preventing jungle (or sylvatic) yellow fever transmission.

Personal preventive measures such as clothing minimizing skin exposure and repellents are recommended to avoid mosquito bites. The use of insecticide-treated bed nets is limited by the fact that Aedes mosquitos bite during the daytime.

EPIDEMIC PREPAREDNESS AND RESPONSE

Prompt detection of yellow fever and rapid response through emergency vaccination campaigns are essential for controlling outbreaks. However, underreporting is a concern – the true number of cases is estimated to be 10 to 250 times what is now being reported.

WHO recommends that every at-risk country have at least one national laboratory where basic yellow fever blood tests can be performed. A confirmed case of yellow fever in an unvaccinated population is considered an outbreak. A confirmed case in any context must be fully investigated. Investigation teams must assess and respond to the outbreak with both emergency measures and longer-term immunization plans.

EPIDEMIOLOGY

Yellow fever is common in tropical and subtropical areas of South America and Africa. Worldwide, about 600 million people live in endemic areas. The WHO estimates 200 000 cases of yellow fever worldwide each year. About 15% of people infected with yellow fever progress to a severe form of the illness, and up to half of those will die, as there is no cure for yellow fever.

AFRICA

An estimated 90% of yellow fever infections occur on the African continent. In 2016, a large outbreak originated in Angola and spread to neighboring countries before being contained by a massive vaccination campaign. In March and April 2016, 11 imported cases of the Angola genotype in unvaccinated Chinese nationals were reported in China, the first appearance of the disease in Asia in recorded history.

Phylogenetic analysis has identified seven genotypes of yellow fever viruses, and they are assumed to be differently adapted to humans and the vector A. aegypti. Five genotypes (Angola, Central/East Africa, East Africa, West Africa I, and West Africa II) occur only in Africa. West Africa genotype I am found in Nigeria and the surrounding region. West Africa genotype I appear to be especially infectious, as it is often associated with major outbreaks. The three genotypes found outside of Nigeria and Angola occur in areas where outbreaks are rare. Two outbreaks, in Kenya (1992–1993) and Sudan (2003 and 2005), involved the East African genotype, which had remained undetected in the previous 40 years.

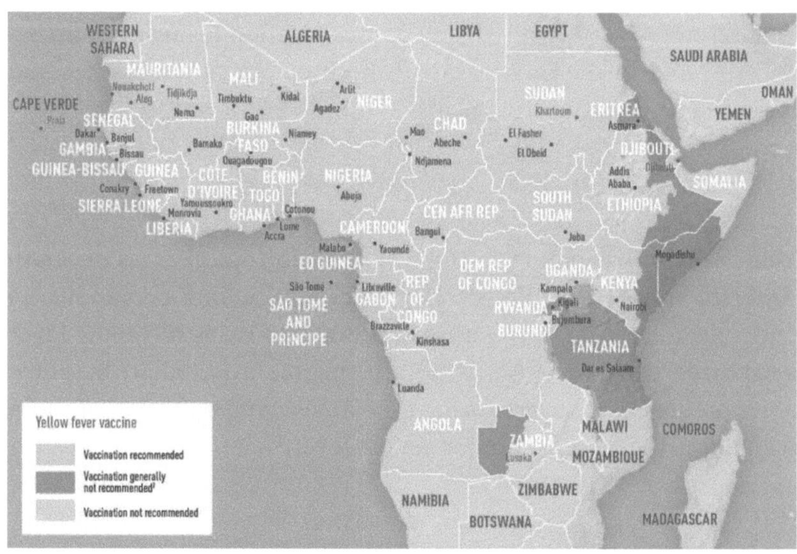

Fig. 7.2 Area with risk of Yellow Fever in Africa

SOUTH AMERICA

In South America, two genotypes have been identified (South American genotypes I and II). Based on phylogenetic analysis these two genotypes appear to have originated in West Africa and were first introduced into Brazil. The date of introduction of the predecessor African genotype which gave rise to the South

American genotypes appears to be 1822 (95% confidence interval 1701 to 1911). The historical record shows an outbreak of yellow fever occurred in Recife, Brazil, between 1685 and 1690. The disease seems to have disappeared, with the next outbreak occurring in 1849. It was likely introduced with the trafficking of slaves through the slave trade from Africa. Genotype I has been divided into five subclades, A through E.

In late 2016, a large outbreak began in Minas Gerais state of Brazil that was characterized as a sylvan or jungle epizootic. It began as an outbreak in brown howler monkeys, which serve as a sentinel species for yellow fever, that then spread to men working in the jungle. No cases had been transmitted between humans by the A. aegypti mosquito, which can sustain urban outbreaks that can spread rapidly. In April 2017, the sylvan outbreak continued moving toward the Brazilian coast, where most people were unvaccinated. By the end of May the outbreak appeared to be declining after more than 3,000 suspected cases, 758 confirmed and 264 deaths confirmed to be yellow fever. The Health Ministry launched a vaccination campaign and was concerned about its spread during the Carnival season in February and March. The CDC issued a Level 2 alert (practice enhanced precautions.)

A Bayesian analysis of genotypes I and II has shown that genotype I account for virtually all the current infections in Brazil, Colombia, Venezuela, and Trinidad and Tobago, while genotype II accounted for all cases in Peru. Genotype I originated in the northern Brazilian region around 1908 (95% highest posterior density interval [HPD]: 1870–1936). Genotype II originated in Peru in 1920 (95% HPD: 1867–1958). The estimated rate of mutation for both genotypes was about 5 × 10–4 substitutions/site/year, similar to that of other RNA viruses.

ASIA

The main vector (A. aegypti) also occurs in tropical and subtropical regions of Asia, the Pacific, and Australia, but yellow fever has never occurred there until jet travel introduced 11 cases from the 2016 Angola and DR Congo yellow fever outbreak in Africa. Proposed explanations include:

That the strains of the mosquito in the east are less able to transmit yellow fever virus.

That immunity is present in the populations because of other diseases caused by related viruses (for example, dengue).

That the disease was never introduced because the shipping trade was insufficient.

But none is considered satisfactory. Another proposal is the absence of slave trade to Asia on the scale of that to the Americas. The trans-Atlantic slave trade probably introduced yellow fever into the Western Hemisphere from Africa.

HISTORY

The evolutionary origins of yellow fever most likely lie in Africa, with the transmission of the disease from nonhuman primates to humans. The virus is thought to have originated in East or Central Africa and spread from there to West Africa. As it was endemic in Africa, local populations had developed some immunity to it. When an outbreak of yellow fever would occur in an African community where colonists resided, most Europeans died, while the indigenous Africans usually developed nonlethal symptoms resembling influenza. This phenomenon, in which certain populations develop immunity to yellow fever due to prolonged exposure in their childhood, is known as acquired immunity. The virus, as well as the vector A. aegypti, were probably transferred to North and South America with the trafficking of slaves from Africa, part of the Columbian Exchange following European exploration and colonization.

The first definitive outbreak of yellow fever in the New World was in 1647 on the island of Barbados. An outbreak was recorded by Spanish colonists in 1648 in the Yucatán Peninsula, where the indigenous Mayan people called the illness xekik ("blood vomit").

In 1685, Brazil suffered its first epidemic in Recife. The first mention of the disease by the name "yellow fever" occurred in 1744. McNeill argues that the environmental and ecological disruption caused by the introduction of sugar plantations created the conditions for mosquito and viral reproduction and subsequent outbreaks of yellow fever. Deforestation reduced populations of insectivorous birds and other creatures that fed on mosquitoes and their eggs.

In Colonial times and during the Napoleonic Wars, the West Indies were known as a particularly dangerous posting for soldiers due to yellow fever being endemic in the area. The mortality rate in British garrisons in Jamaica was seven times that of garrisons in Canada, mostly because of yellow fever and other tropical diseases. Both English and French forces posted there were seriously affected by the "yellow jack". Wanting to regain control of the lucrative sugar trade in Saint-Domingue (Hispaniola), and with an eye on regaining France's New World empire, Napoleon sent an army under the command of his brother-in-law General Charles Leclerc to Saint-Domingue to seize control after a slave revolt. The historian J. R. McNeill asserts that yellow fever accounted for about 35,000 to 45,000 casualties of these forces during the fighting. Only one-third of the French troops survived for withdrawal and return to France. Napoleon gave up on the island and his plans for North America, selling the Louisiana Purchase to the US in 1803. In 1804, Haiti proclaimed its independence as the second republic in the Western Hemisphere. Considerable debate exists over whether the number of deaths caused by disease in the Haitian Revolution was exaggerated.

Although yellow fever is most prevalent in tropical-like climates, the northern United States was not exempted from the fever. The first outbreak in English-speaking North America occurred in New York City in 1668. English colonists in Philadelphia and the French in the Mississippi River Valley recorded major outbreaks in 1669, as well as additional yellow fever epidemics in Philadelphia, Baltimore, and New York City in the 18th and 19th centuries. The disease traveled along steamboat routes from New Orleans, causing some 100,000–150,000 deaths in total. The yellow fever epidemic of 1793 in Philadelphia, which was then the capital of the United States, resulted in the deaths of several thousand people, more than 9% of the population. One of these tragic deaths was James Hutchinson, a physician helping to treat the population of the city. The national government fled the city to Trenton, New Jersey, including President George Washington.

The southern city of New Orleans was plagued with major epidemics during the 19th century, most notably in 1833 and 1853. A major epidemic occurred in both New Orleans and Shreveport, Louisiana in 1873. Its residents called the disease "yellow jack". Urban epidemics continued in the United States until 1905, with the last outbreak affecting New Orleans.

At least 25 major outbreaks took place in the Americas during the 18th and 19th centuries, including particularly serious ones in Cartagena, Chile, in 1741; Cuba in 1762 and 1900; Santo Domingo in 1803; and Memphis, Tennessee, in 1878.

In the early nineteenth century, the prevalence of yellow fever in the Caribbean "led to serious health problems" and alarmed the United States Navy as numerous deaths and sickness curtailed naval operations and destroyed morale. A tragic episode began in April 1822 when the frigate USS Macedonian left Boston and became part of Commodore James Biddle's West India Squadron. Unbeknownst to all, they were about to embark on a cruise to disaster and their assignment "would prove a cruise through hell". Secretary of the Navy Smith Thompson had assigned the squadron to guard United States merchant shipping and suppress piracy. During their time on deployment from 26 May to 3 August 1822, seventy-six of the Macedonian's officers and men died, including Dr. John Cadle, Surgeon USN. Seventy-four of these deaths were attributed to yellow fever. Biddle reported that another fifty-two of his crew were on the sick list. In their report to the Secretary of the Navy, Biddle and Surgeon's Mate Dr. Charles Chase stated the cause as "fever". As a consequence of this loss, Biddle noted that his squadron was forced to return to Norfolk Navy Yard early. Upon arrival, the Macedonian's crew were provided medical care and quarantined at Craney Island, Virginia.

In 1853, Cloutierville, Louisiana, had a late-summer outbreak of yellow fever that quickly killed 68 of the 91 inhabitants. A local doctor concluded that some unspecified infectious agent had arrived in a package from New Orleans. In 1854, 650 residents of Savannah, Georgia, died from yellow fever. In 1858, St. Matthew's German Evangelical Lutheran Church in Charleston, South Carolina, suffered 308 yellow fever deaths, reducing the congregation by half. A ship carrying persons infected with the virus arrived in Hampton Roads in southeastern Virginia in June 1855. The disease spread quickly through the community, eventually killing over 3,000 people, mostly residents of Norfolk and Portsmouth. In 1873, Shreveport, Louisiana, lost 759 citizens in 80 days to a yellow fever epidemic, with over 400 additional victims eventually succumbing. The total death toll from August through November was approximately 1,200.

In 1878, about 20,000 people died in a widespread epidemic in the Mississippi River Valley. That year, Memphis had an unusually large amount of rain, which led to an increase in the mosquito population. The result was a huge epidemic of yellow fever. The steamship John D. Porter took people fleeing Memphis northward in hopes of escaping the disease, but passengers were not allowed to disembark due to concerns of spreading yellow fever. The ship roamed the Mississippi River for the next two months before unloading her passengers.

Major outbreaks have also occurred in southern Europe. Gibraltar lost many lives to outbreaks in 1804, 1814, and 1828. Barcelona suffered the loss of several thousand citizens during an outbreak in 1821. The Duke de Richelieu deployed 30,000 French troops to the border between France and Spain in the Pyrenees Mountains, to establish a cordon sanitaire to prevent the epidemic from spreading from Spain into France.

KEY FACTS

Yellow fever is an acute viral hemorrhagic disease transmitted by infected mosquitoes. The "yellow" in the name refers to jaundice that affects some patients.

Symptoms of yellow fever include fever, headache, jaundice, muscle pain, nausea, vomiting, and fatigue.

A small proportion of patients who contract the virus develop severe symptoms and approximately half of those die within 7 to 10 days.

The virus is endemic in tropical areas of Africa and Central and South America.

Large epidemics of yellow fever occur when infected people introduce the virus into heavily populated areas with high mosquito density and where most people have little or no immunity, due to lack of vaccination. In these conditions, infected mosquitoes of the Aedes aegypti species transmit the virus from person to person.

Yellow fever is prevented by an extremely effective vaccine, which is safe and affordable. A single dose of yellow fever vaccine is sufficient to grant sustained immunity and life-long protection against yellow fever disease. A booster dose of the vaccine is not needed. The vaccine provides effective immunity within 10 days for 80-100% of people vaccinated, and within 30 days for more than 99% of people vaccinated.

Good supportive treatment in hospitals improves survival rates. There is currently no specific anti-viral drug for yellow fever.

The Eliminate Yellow fever Epidemics (EYE) Strategy launched in 2017 is an unprecedented initiative. With more than 50 partners involved, the EYE partnership supports 40 at-risk countries in Africa and the Americas to prevent, detect, and respond to yellow fever suspected cases and outbreaks. The partnership aims at protecting at-risk populations, preventing international spread, and containing outbreaks rapidly. By 2026, it is expected that more than 1 billion people will be protected against the disease.

CHAPTER EIGHT

THE EBOLA VIRUS

Ebola, also known as Ebola virus disease (EVD) and Ebola hemorrhagic fever (EHF), is a viral hemorrhagic fever in humans and other primates, caused by ebolaviruses. Symptoms typically start anywhere between two days and three weeks after becoming infected with the virus. The first symptoms are usually fever, sore throat, muscle pain, and headaches. These are usually followed by vomiting, diarrhea, rash, and decreased liver and kidney function, at which point, some people begin to bleed both internally and externally. The disease kills between 25% and 90% of those infected—about 50% on average. Death is often due to shock from fluid loss and typically occurs between six and 16 days after the first symptoms appear.

The Ebola virus causes an acute, serious illness that is often fatal if untreated. EVD first appeared in 1976 in 2 simultaneous outbreaks, one in what is now Nzara, South Sudan, and the other in Yambuku, DRC. The latter occurred in a village near the Ebola River, from which the disease takes its name. The 2014–2016 outbreak in West Africa was the largest Ebola outbreak since the virus was first discovered in 1976. The outbreak started in Guinea and then moved across land borders to Sierra Leone and Liberia.

The virus family Filoviridae includes three genera: Cuevavirus, Marburgvirus, and Ebolavirus. Within the genus Ebolavirus, six species have been identified: Zaire, Bundibugyo, Sudan, Taï Forest, Reston, and Bombali.

The virus spreads through direct contact with body fluids, such as blood from infected humans or other animals, or from contact with items that have recently been contaminated with infected body fluids. There have been no documented cases, either in nature or under laboratory conditions, of the disease spreading through the air between humans or other primates. After a person recovers from Ebola, their semen or breast milk may continue to carry the virus for anywhere between several weeks to several months. Fruit bats are believed to be the normal carrier in nature; they are able to spread the virus without being affected by it. The symptoms of Ebola may resemble those of several other diseases, including malaria, cholera, typhoid fever, meningitis, and other viral hemorrhagic fevers. Diagnosis is confirmed by testing blood samples for the presence of viral RNA, viral antibodies, or the virus itself.

Control of outbreaks requires coordinated medical services and community engagement, including rapid detection, contact tracing of those exposed, quick access to laboratory services, care for those infected, and proper disposal of the dead through cremation or burial. Samples of body fluids and tissues from people with the disease should be handled with extreme caution. Prevention measures include wearing proper protective clothing and washing hands when around a person with the disease, and limiting the spread of the disease from infected animals to humans—by wearing protective clothing while handling potentially infected bushmeat, and by cooking bushmeat thoroughly before eating it. An Ebola vaccine was approved in the United States in December 2019. While there is no approved treatment for Ebola as of 2019, two treatments (atoltivimab/maftivimab/odesivimab and ansuvimab) are associated with improved outcomes. Supportive efforts also improve outcomes. These include oral rehydration therapy (drinking slightly sweetened and salty water) or giving intravenous fluids and treating symptoms. In October 2020, Atoltivimab/maftivimab/odesivimab (Inmazeb) was approved for medical use in the United States to treat the disease caused by Zaire ebolavirus.

The disease was first identified in 1976, in two simultaneous outbreaks: one in Nzara (a town in South Sudan) and the other in Yambuku (the Democratic Republic of the Congo), a village near the Ebola River, from which the disease takes its name. Ebola outbreaks occur intermittently in tropical regions of sub-Saharan Africa. Between 1976 and 2012, according to the World Health Organization, there were 24 outbreaks of Ebola resulting in a total of 2,387 cases and 1,590 deaths. The largest Ebola outbreak to date was an epidemic in West Africa from December 2013 to January 2016, with 28,646 cases and 11,323 deaths. On 29 March 2016, it was declared to no longer be an emergency. Other outbreaks in Africa began in the Democratic Republic of the Congo in May 2017 and 2018. In July 2019, the World Health Organization declared the Congo Ebola outbreak a world health emergency.

SIGNS AND SYMPTOMS

The incubation period, that is, the time interval from infection with the virus to onset of symptoms is from 2 to 21 days. A person infected with Ebola cannot spread the disease until they develop symptoms.

Symptoms of EVD can be sudden and include:

Fever, Fatigue, Muscle pain, Headache, Sore throat

This is followed by:

Vomiting, Diarrhoea, Rash, Symptoms of impaired kidney and liver function.

In some cases, both internal and external bleeding (for example, oozing from the gums, or blood in the stools). Laboratory findings include low white blood cell and platelet counts and elevated liver enzymes.

ONSET

The length of time between exposure to the virus and the development of symptoms (incubation period) is between two and

21 days, and usually between four and ten days. However, recent estimates based on mathematical models predict that around 5% of cases may take longer than 21 days to develop.

Symptoms usually begin with a sudden influenza-like stage characterized by fatigue, fever, weakness, decreased appetite, muscular pain, joint pain, headache, and sore throat. The fever is usually higher than 38.3 °C (101 °F). This is often followed by nausea, vomiting, diarrhea, abdominal pain, and sometimes hiccups. The combination of severe vomiting and diarrhea often leads to severe dehydration. Next, shortness of breath and chest pain may occur, along with swelling, headaches, and confusion. In about half of the cases, the skin may develop a maculopapular rash, a flat red area covered with small bumps, five to seven days after symptoms begin.

BLEEDING

In some cases, internal and external bleeding may occur. This typically begins five to seven days after the first symptoms. All infected people show some decreased blood clotting. Bleeding from mucous membranes or from sites of needle punctures has been reported in 40–50% of cases. This may cause vomiting blood, coughing up blood, or blood in the stool. Bleeding into the skin may create petechiae, purpura, ecchymoses, or hematomas (especially around needle injection sites). Bleeding into the whites of the eyes may also occur. Heavy bleeding is uncommon; if it occurs, it is usually in the gastrointestinal tract. The incidence of bleeding into the gastrointestinal tract was reported to be ~58% in the 2001 outbreak in Gabon, but in the 2014–15 outbreak in the US it was ~18%, possibly due to improved prevention of disseminated intravascular coagulation.

RECOVERY AND DEATH

Recovery may begin between seven and 14 days after the first symptoms. Death, if it occurs, follows typically six to sixteen days from first symptoms and is often due to shock from fluid loss. In general, bleeding often indicates a worse outcome, and blood loss may result in death. People are often in a coma near the end of life.

Those who survive often have ongoing muscular and joint pain, liver inflammation, and decreased hearing, and may have continued tiredness, continued weakness, decreased appetite, and difficulty returning to pre-illness weight. Problems with vision may develop. It is recommended that survivors of EVD wear condoms for at least twelve months after initial infection or until the semen of male survivors tests negative for Ebola virus on two separate occasions.

Survivors develop antibodies against Ebola that last at least 10 years, but it is unclear whether they are immune to additional infections.

CAUSE

EVD in humans is caused by four of five viruses of the genus Ebolavirus. The four are Bundibugyo virus (BDBV), Sudan virus (SUDV), Taï Forest virus (TAFV) and one simply called Ebola virus (EBOV, formerly Zaire Ebola virus). EBOV, species Zaire ebolavirus, is the most dangerous of the known EVD-causing viruses and is responsible for the largest number of outbreaks. The fifth virus, Reston virus (RESTV), is not thought to cause disease in humans but has caused disease in other primates. All five viruses are closely related to marburgviruses.

VIROLOGY

Ebolaviruses contain single-stranded, non-infectious RNA genomes. Ebolavirus genomes contain seven genes including 3‘-UTR-NP-VP35-VP40-GP-VP30-VP24-L-5’-UTR. The genomes of the five different ebolaviruses (BDBV, EBOV, RESTV, SUDV, and TAFV) differ in sequence, and the number and location of gene overlap. As with all filoviruses, ebolavirus virions are filamentous particles that may appear in the shape of a shepherd's crook, of a "U" or of a "6," and they may be coiled, toroid, or branched. In general, ebolavirions are 80 nanometers (nm) in width and maybe as long as 14,000 nm.

Their life cycle is thought to begin with a virion attaching to specific cell-surface receptors such as C-type lectins, DC-SIGN, or integrins, which is followed by fusion of the viral envelope with cellular membranes. The virions are taken up by the cell then travel to acidic endosomes and lysosomes where the viral envelope glycoprotein GP is cleaved. This processing appears to allow the virus to bind to cellular proteins enabling it to fuse with internal cellular membranes and release the viral nucleocapsid. The Ebolavirus structural glycoprotein (known as GP1,2) is responsible for the virus's ability to bind to and infect targeted cells. The viral RNA polymerase, encoded by the L gene, partially uncoats the nucleocapsid and transcribes the genes into positive-strand mRNAs, which are then translated into structural and nonstructural proteins. The most abundant protein produced is the nucleoprotein, whose concentration in the host cell determines when L switches from gene transcription to genome replication. Replication of the viral genome results in full-length, positive-strand antigenomes that are, in turn, transcribed into genome copies of negative-strand virus progeny. Newly synthesized structural proteins and genomes self-assemble and accumulate near the inside of the cell membrane. Virions bud off from the cell, gaining their envelopes from the cellular membrane from which they bud. The mature progeny particles then infect other cells to repeat the cycle. The genetics of the Ebola virus is difficult to study because of EBOV's virulent characteristics.

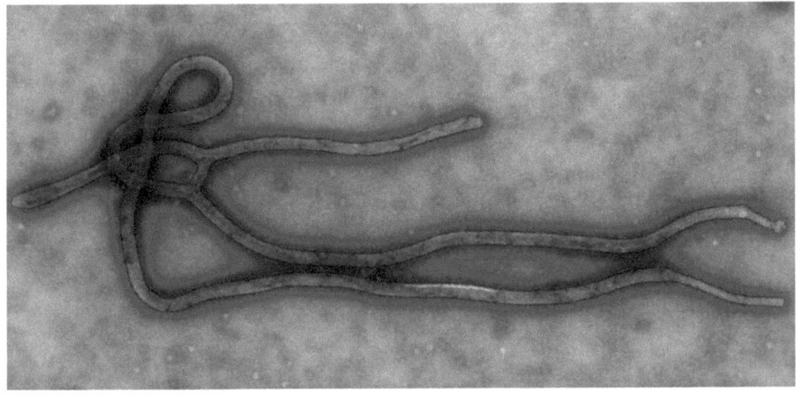

Fig. 8.1 Ebola Virus

TRANSMISSION

It is believed that between people, Ebola disease spreads only by direct contact with the blood or other body fluids of a person who has developed symptoms of the disease. Body fluids that may contain Ebola viruses include saliva, mucus, vomit, feces, sweat, tears, breast milk, urine, and semen. The WHO states that only people who are very sick are able to spread the Ebola disease in saliva, and the virus has not been reported to be transmitted through sweat. Most people spread the virus through blood, feces, and vomit. Entry points for the virus include the nose, mouth, eyes, open wounds, cuts, and abrasions. Ebola may be spread through large droplets; however, this is believed to occur only when a person is very sick. This contamination can happen if a person is splashed with droplets. Contact with surfaces or objects contaminated by the virus, particularly needles and syringes, may also transmit the infection. The virus is able to survive on objects for a few hours in a dried state and can survive for a few days within body fluids outside of a person.

The Ebola virus may be able to persist for more than three months in the semen after recovery, which could lead to infections via sexual intercourse. Virus persistence in semen for over a year has been recorded in a national screening program. Ebola may also occur in the breast milk of women after recovery, and it is not known when it is safe to breastfeed again. The virus was also found in the eye of one patient in 2014, two months after it was cleared from his blood. Otherwise, people who have recovered are not infectious.

The potential for widespread infections in countries with medical systems capable of observing correct medical isolation procedures is considered low. Usually, when someone has symptoms of the disease, they are unable to travel without assistance.

Dead bodies remain infectious; thus, people handling human remains in practices such as traditional burial rituals or more modern processes such as embalming are at risk. 69% of the cases of Ebola infections in Guinea during the 2014 outbreak are believed to have been contracted via unprotected (or unsuitably protected) contact with infected corpses during certain Guinean burial rituals.

Health-care workers treating people with Ebola are at the greatest risk of infection. The risk increases when they do not have appropriate protective clothing such as masks, gowns, gloves, and eye protection; do not wear it properly, or handle contaminated clothing incorrectly. This risk is particularly common in parts of Africa where the disease mostly occurs and health systems function poorly. There has been transmission in hospitals in some African countries that reuse hypodermic needles. Some healthcare centers caring for people with the disease do not have running water. In the United States, the spread to two medical workers treating infected patients prompted criticism of inadequate training and procedures.

Human-to-human transmission of EBOV through the air has not been reported to occur during EVD outbreaks, and airborne transmission has only been demonstrated in very strict laboratory conditions, and then only from pigs to primates, but not from primates to primates. Spread of EBOV by water, or food other than bushmeat has not been observed. No spread by mosquitos or other insects has been reported. Other possible methods of transmission are being studied.

Airborne transmission among humans is theoretically possible due to the presence of Ebola virus particles in saliva, which can be discharged into the air with a cough or sneeze, but observational data from previous epidemics suggests the actual risk of airborne transmission is low. A number of studies examining airborne transmission broadly concluded that transmission from pigs to primates could happen without direct contact because, unlike humans and primates, pigs with EVD get very high ebolavirus concentrations in their lungs, and not their bloodstream. Therefore, pigs with EVD can spread the disease through droplets in the air or on the ground when they sneeze or cough. By contrast, humans and other primates accumulate the virus throughout their bodies and specifically in their blood, but not very much in their lungs. It is believed that this is the reason researchers have observed pig to primate transmission without physical contact, but no evidence has been found of primates being infected without actual contact, even in experiments where infected and uninfected primates shared the same air.

It is thought that fruit bats of the Pteropodidae family are natural Ebola, virus hosts. Ebola is introduced into the human population through close contact with the blood, secretions, organs or other bodily fluids of infected animals such as fruit bats, chimpanzees, gorillas, monkeys, forest antelope or porcupines found ill or dead or in the rainforest.

Ebola then spreads through human-to-human transmission via direct contact (through broken skin or mucous membranes) with:

1. Blood or body fluids of a person who is sick with or has died from Ebola
2. Objects that have been contaminated with body fluids (like blood, feces, vomit) from a person sick with Ebola or the body

of a person who died from Ebola.

Health-care workers have frequently been infected while treating patients with suspected or confirmed EVD. This occurs through close contact with patients when infection control precautions are not strictly practiced. Burial ceremonies that involve direct contact with the body of the deceased can also contribute to the transmission of Ebola. People remain infectious as long as their blood contains the virus.

Pregnant women who get acute Ebola and recover from the disease may still carry the virus in breastmilk, or in pregnancy-related fluids and tissues. This poses a risk of transmission to the baby they carry, and to others. Women who become pregnant after surviving Ebola disease are not at risk of carrying the virus. If a breastfeeding woman who is recovering from Ebola wishes to continue breastfeeding, she should be supported to do so. Her breast milk needs to be tested for Ebola before she can start.

INITIAL CASE

Although it is not entirely clear how Ebola initially spreads from animals to humans, the spread is believed to involve direct contact with an infected wild animal or fruit bat. Besides bats, other wild animals sometimes infected with EBOV include several species of monkeys such as baboons, great apes (chimpanzees and gorillas), and duikers (a species of antelope).

Animals may become infected when they eat fruit partially eaten by bats carrying the virus. Fruit production, animal behavior, and other factors may trigger outbreaks among animal populations.

Evidence indicates that both domestic dogs and pigs can also be infected with EBOV. Dogs do not appear to develop symptoms when they carry the virus, and pigs appear to be able to transmit the virus to at least some primates. Although some dogs in an area in which a human outbreak occurred had antibodies to EBOV, it is unclear whether they played a role in spreading the disease to people.

RESERVOIR

The natural reservoir for Ebola has yet to be confirmed; however, bats are considered to be the most likely candidate. Three types of fruit bats (Hypsignathus monstrous, Epomops franqueti, and Myonycteris torquata) were found to possibly carry the virus without getting sick. As of 2013, whether other animals are involved in its spread is not known. Plants, arthropods, rodents, and birds have also been considered possible viral reservoirs.

Bats were known to roost in the cotton factory in which the first cases of the 1976 and 1979 outbreaks were observed, and they have also been implicated in Marburg virus infections in 1975 and 1980. Of 24 plant and 19 vertebrate species experimentally inoculated with EBOV, only bats became infected. The bats displayed no clinical signs of disease, which is considered evidence that these bats are a reservoir species of EBOV. In a 2002–2003 survey of 1,030 animals including 679 bats from Gabon and the Republic of the Congo, immunoglobulin G (IgG) immune defense molecules indicative of Ebola infection were found in three bat species; at various periods of study, between 2.2 and 22.6% of bats were found to contain both RNA sequences and IgG molecules indicating Ebola infection. Antibodies against Zaire and Reston viruses have been found in fruit bats in Bangladesh, suggesting that these bats are also potential hosts of the virus and that the filoviruses are present in Asia.

Between 1976 and 1998, in 30,000 mammals, birds, reptiles, amphibians, and arthropods sampled from regions of EBOV outbreaks, no Ebola virus was detected apart from some genetic traces found in six rodents (belonging to the species Mus setulosus and Praomys) and one shrew (Sylvisorex ollula) collected from the Central African Republic. However, further research efforts have not confirmed rodents as a reservoir. Traces of EBOV were detected in the carcasses of gorillas and chimpanzees during outbreaks in

2001 and 2003, which later became the source of human infections. However, the high rates of death in these species resulting from EBOV infection make it unlikely that these species represent a natural reservoir for the virus.

Deforestation has been mentioned as a possible contributor to recent outbreaks, including the West African Ebola virus epidemic. Index cases of EVD have often been close to recently deforested lands.

PATHOPHYSIOLOGY

Like other filoviruses, EBOV replicates very efficiently in many cells, producing large amounts of virus in monocytes, macrophages, dendritic cells, and other cells including liver cells, fibroblasts, and adrenal gland cells. Viral replication triggers high levels of inflammatory chemical signals and leads to a septic state.

EBOV is thought to infect humans through contact with mucous membranes or skin breaks. After infection, endothelial cells (cells lining the inside of blood vessels), liver cells, and several types of immune cells such as macrophages, monocytes, and dendritic cells are the main targets of attack. Following infection, immune cells carry the virus to nearby lymph nodes where further reproduction of the virus takes place. From there the virus can enter the bloodstream and lymphatic system and spread throughout the body. Macrophages are the first cells infected with the virus and this infection results in programmed cell death. Other types of white blood cells, such as lymphocytes, also undergo programmed cell death leading to an abnormally low concentration of lymphocytes in the blood. This contributes to the weakened immune response seen in those infected with EBOV.

Endothelial cells may be infected within three days after exposure to the virus. The breakdown of endothelial cells leading to blood vessel injury can be attributed to EBOV glycoproteins. This damage occurs due to the synthesis of the Ebola virus glycoprotein (GP), which reduces the availability of specific integrins responsible for cell adhesion to the intercellular structure and causes liver damage, leading to improper clotting. The widespread bleeding that occurs in affected people causes swelling and shock due to loss of blood volume. The dysfunctional bleeding and clotting commonly seen in EVD have been attributed to increased activation of the extrinsic pathway of the coagulation cascade due to excessive tissue factor production by macrophages and monocytes.

After infection, a secreted glycoprotein, small soluble glycoprotein (sGP or GP) is synthesized. EBOV replication overwhelms protein synthesis of infected cells and the host immune defenses. The GP forms a trimeric complex, which tethers the virus to the endothelial cells. The sGP forms a dimeric protein that interferes with the signaling of neutrophils, another type of white blood cell. This enables the virus to evade the immune system by inhibiting the early steps of neutrophil activation.

IMMUNE SYSTEM EVASION

Filoviral infection also interferes with the proper functioning of the innate immune system. EBOV proteins blunt the human immune system's response to viral infections by interfering with the cells' ability to produce and respond to interferon proteins such as interferon-alpha, interferon-beta, and interferon-gamma.

The VP24 and VP35 structural proteins of EBOV play a key role in this interference. When a cell is infected with EBOV, receptors located in the cell's cytosol (such as RIG-I and MDA5) or outside of the cytosol (such as Toll-like receptor 3 (TLR3), TLR7, TLR8, and TLR9) recognize infectious molecules associated with the virus. On TLR activation, proteins including interferon regulatory factor 3 and interferon regulatory factor 7 trigger a signaling cascade that leads to the expression of type 1 interferons. The type 1 interferons are then released and bind to the IFNAR1 and IFNAR2 receptors expressed on the surface of a neighboring cell. Once interferon has bound to its receptors on the neighboring cell, the signaling proteins STAT1 and STAT2 are activated and move to the cell's nucleus. This triggers the expression of interferon-stimulated genes, which code for proteins with antiviral properties. EBOV's V24 protein blocks the production of these antiviral proteins by preventing the STAT1 signaling protein in the neighboring cell from entering the nucleus. The VP35 protein directly inhibits the production of interferon-beta. By inhibiting these immune responses, EBOV may quickly spread throughout the body.

DIAGNOSIS

It can be difficult to clinically distinguish EVD from other infectious diseases such as malaria, typhoid fever, and meningitis. Many symptoms of pregnancy and Ebola disease are also quite similar. Because of risks to the pregnancy, pregnant women should ideally be tested rapidly if Ebola is suspected.

Confirmation that symptoms are caused by Ebola virus infection are made using the following diagnostic methods:

1. Antibody-capture enzyme-linked immunosorbent assay (ELISA)
2. Antigen-capture detection tests
3. Serum neutralization test
4. Reverse transcriptase-polymerase chain reaction (RT-PCR) assay
5. Electron microscopy
6. Virus isolation by cell culture.

Careful consideration should be given to the selection of diagnostic tests, which take into account technical specifications, disease incidence and prevalence, and social and medical implications of test results. It is strongly recommended that diagnostic tests, which have undergone an independent and international evaluation, be considered for use.

LABORATORY TESTING

Possible non-specific laboratory indicators of EVD include a low platelet count; an initially decreased white blood cell count followed by an increased white blood cell count; elevated levels of the liver enzymes alanine aminotransferase (ALT) and aspartate aminotransferase (AST); and abnormalities in blood clotting often consistent with disseminated intravascular coagulation (DIC) such as a prolonged prothrombin time, partial thromboplastin time, and bleeding time. Filovirions such as EBOV may be identified by their unique filamentous shapes in cell cultures examined with electron microscopy.

The specific diagnosis of EVD is confirmed by isolating the virus, detecting its RNA or proteins, or detecting antibodies against the virus in a person's blood. Isolating the virus by cell culture, detecting the viral RNA by polymerase chain reaction (PCR), and detecting proteins by enzyme-linked immunosorbent assay (ELISA) are methods best used in the early stages of the disease and also for detecting the virus in human remains. Detecting antibodies against the virus is most reliable in the later stages of the disease and in those who recover. IgM antibodies are detectable two days after symptom onset and IgG antibodies can be detected six to 18 days after symptom onset. During an outbreak, isolation of the virus with cell culture methods is often not feasible. Infield or mobile hospitals, the most common and sensitive diagnostic methods are real-time PCR and ELISA. In 2014, with new mobile testing facilities deployed in parts of Liberia, test results were obtained 3–5 hours after sample submission. In 2015, a rapid antigen test that gives results in 15 minutes was approved for use by WHO. It is able to confirm Ebola in 92% of those affected and rule it out in 85% of those not affected.

DIFFERENTIAL DIAGNOSIS

Early symptoms of EVD may be similar to those of other diseases common in Africa, including malaria and dengue fever. The symptoms are also similar to those of other viral hemorrhagic fevers such as Marburg virus disease, Crimean–Congo hemorrhagic fever, and Lassa fever.

The complete differential diagnosis is extensive and requires consideration of many other infectious diseases such as typhoid fever, shigellosis, rickettsial diseases, cholera, sepsis, borreliosis, EHEC enteritis, leptospirosis, scrub typhus, plague, fever, candidiasis, histoplasmosis, trypanosomiasis, visceral leishmaniasis, measles, and viral hepatitis among others.

Non-infectious diseases that may result in symptoms similar to those of EVD include acute promyelocytic leukemia, hemolytic uraemic syndrome, snake envenomation, clotting factor deficiencies/platelet disorders, thrombotic thrombocytopenic purpura, hereditary hemorrhagic telangiectasia, Kawasaki disease, and warfarin poisoning.

EPIDEMIOLOGY

The disease typically occurs in outbreaks in tropical regions of Sub-Saharan Africa. From 1976 (when it was first identified) through 2013, the WHO reported 2,387 confirmed cases with 1,590 overall fatalities. The largest outbreak to date was the Ebola virus epidemic in West Africa, which caused a large number of deaths in Guinea and Liberia.

1976

SUDAN

The first known outbreak of EVD was identified only after the fact. It occurred between June and November 1976, in Nzara, South Sudan (then part of Sudan), and was caused by the Sudan virus

(SUDV). The Sudan outbreak infected 284 people and killed 151. The first identifiable case in Sudan occurred on 27 June in a storekeeper in a cotton factory in Nzara, who was hospitalized on 30 June and died on 6 July. Although the WHO medical staff involved in the Sudan outbreak knew that they were dealing with a heretofore unknown disease, the actual "positive identification" process and the naming of the virus did not occur until some months later in Zaire.

ZAIRE

On 26 August 1976, the second outbreak of EVD began in Yambuku, a small rural village in Mongala District in northern Zaire (now known as the Democratic Republic of the Congo). This outbreak was caused by EBOV, formerly designated Zaire ebolavirus, a different member of the genus Ebolavirus than in the first Sudan outbreak. The first person infected with the disease was the village school's headmaster Mabalo Lokela, who began displaying symptoms on 26 August 1976. Lokela had returned from a trip to Northern Zaire near the border of the Central African Republic, after visiting the Ebola River between 12 and 22 August. He was originally believed to have malaria and was given quinine. However, his symptoms continued to worsen, and he was admitted to Yambuku Mission Hospital on 5 September. Lokela died on 8 September 14 days after he began displaying symptoms.

Soon after Lokela's death, others who had been in contact with him also died, and people in Yambuku began to panic. The country's Minister of Health and Zaire President Mobutu Sese Seko declared the entire region, including Yambuku and the country's capital, Kinshasa, a quarantine zone. No one was permitted to enter or leave the area, and roads, waterways, and airfields were placed under martial law. Schools, businesses, and social organizations were closed. The initial response was led by Congolese doctors, including Jean-Jacques Muyembe-Tamfum, one of the discoverers of Ebola. Muyembe took a blood sample from a Belgian nun; this sample would eventually be used by Peter Piot to identify the previously unknown Ebola virus. Muyembe was also the first scientist to come into direct contact with the disease and survive. Researchers from the Centers for Disease Control and Prevention (CDC), including Piot, co-discoverer of Ebola, later arrived to assess the effects of the outbreak, observing that "the whole region was in a panic."

Piot concluded that Belgian nuns had inadvertently started the epidemic by giving unnecessary vitamin injections to pregnant women without sterilizing the syringes and needles. The outbreak lasted 26 days and the quarantine lasted two weeks. Researchers speculated that the disease disappeared due to the precautions taken by locals, the quarantine of the area, and discontinuing the injections.

During this outbreak, Ngoy Mushola recorded the first clinical description of EVD in Yambuku, where he wrote the following in his daily log: "The illness is characterized with a high temperature of about 39 °C (102 °F), haematemesis, diarrhea with blood, retrosternal abdominal pain, prostration with 'heavy' articulations, and rapid evolution death after a mean of three days."

The virus responsible for the initial outbreak, first thought to be the Marburg virus, was later identified as a new type of virus related to the genus Marburgvirus. Virus strain samples isolated from both outbreaks were named "Ebola virus" after the Ebola River, near the first-identified viral outbreak site in Zaire. Reports conflict about who initially coined the name: either Karl Johnson of the American CDC team or Belgian researchers. Subsequently, a number of other cases were reported, almost all centered on the Yambuku mission hospital or close contacts of another case. In all, 318 cases and 280 deaths (an 88% fatality rate) occurred in Zaire. Although the two outbreaks were at first believed connected, scientists later realized that they were caused by two distinct ebolaviruses, SUDV and EBOV.

1995-2014

The second major outbreak occurred in Zaire (now the Democratic Republic of the Congo, DRC), in 1995, affecting 315 and killing 254.

In 2000, Uganda had an outbreak infecting 425 and killing 224; in this case, the Sudan virus was found to be the Ebola species responsible for the outbreak.

In 2003, an outbreak in the DRC infected 143 and killed 128, a 90% death rate, the highest of a genus Ebola virus outbreak to date.

In 2004, a Russian scientist died from Ebola after sticking herself with an infected needle.

Between April and August 2007, a fever epidemic in a four-village region of the DRC was confirmed in September to have been cases of Ebola. Many people who attended the recent funeral of a local village chief died. The 2007 outbreak eventually infected 264 individuals and killed 187.

On 30 November 2007, the Uganda Ministry of Health confirmed an outbreak of Ebola in the Bundibugyo District in Western Uganda. After confirming samples tested by the United States National Reference Laboratories and the Centers for Disease Control, the World Health Organization (WHO) confirmed the presence of a new species of genus Ebolavirus, which was tentatively named Bundibugyo. The WHO reported 149 cases of this new strain and 37 of those led to deaths.

The WHO confirmed two small outbreaks in Uganda in 2012, both caused by the Sudan variant. The first outbreak affected seven people, killing four, and the second affected 24, killing 17.

On 17 August 2012, the Ministry of Health of the DRC reported an outbreak of the Ebola-Bundibugyo variant in the eastern region. Other than its discovery in 2007, this was the only time that this variant has been identified as responsible for an outbreak. The WHO revealed that the virus had sickened 57 people and killed 29. The probable cause of the outbreak was tainted bush meat hunted by local villagers around the towns of Isiro and Viadana.

In 2014, an outbreak occurred in the DRC. Genome-sequencing showed that this outbreak was not related to the 2014–15 West Africa Ebola virus outbreak, but was the same EBOV species, the Zaire species. It began in August 2014 and was declared over in November with 66 cases and 49 deaths. This was the 7th outbreak in the DRC, three of which occurred during the period when the country was known as Zaire.

2013-2016 WEST AFRICA

In March 2014, the World Health Organization (WHO) reported a major Ebola outbreak in Guinea, a West African nation. Researchers tracked the outbreak to a one-year-old child who died in December 2013. The disease rapidly spread to the neighboring countries of Liberia and Sierra Leone. It was the largest Ebola outbreak ever documented, and the first recorded in the region. On 8 August 2014, the WHO declared the epidemic an international public health emergency. Urging the world to offer aid to the affected regions, its Director-General said, "Countries affected to date simply do not have the capacity to manage an outbreak of this size and complexity on their own. I urge the international community to provide this support on the most urgent basis possible." By mid-August 2014, Doctors Without Borders reported the situation in Liberia's capital, Monrovia, was "catastrophic" and "deteriorating daily". They reported that fears of Ebola among staff members and patients had shut down much of the city's health system, leaving many people without medical treatment for other conditions. In a 26 September statement, WHO said, "The Ebola epidemic ravaging parts of West Africa is the most severe acute public health emergency seen in modern times. Never before in recorded history has a biosafety level four pathogen infected so many people so quickly, over such a broad geographical area, for so long."

Intense contact tracing and strict isolation largely prevented the further spread of the disease in the countries that had imported cases.

It caused significant mortality, with a considerable case fatality rate. By the end of the epidemic, 28,616 people had been infected; of these, 11,310 had died, for a case-fatality rate of 40%. As of 8 May 2016, 28,646 suspected cases and 11,323 deaths were reported; however, the WHO said that these numbers may be underestimated. Because they work closely with the body fluids of infected patients, healthcare workers were especially vulnerable to infection; in August 2014, the WHO reported that 10% of the dead were healthcare workers.

In September 2014, it was estimated that the countries' capacity for treating Ebola patients was insufficient by the equivalent of 2,122 beds; by December there were a sufficient number of beds to treat and isolate all reported Ebola cases, although the uneven distribution of cases was causing serious shortfalls in some areas. On 28 January 2015, the WHO reported that for the first time since the week ending 29 June 2014, there had been fewer than 100 new confirmed cases reported in a week in the three most-affected countries. The response to the epidemic then moved to a second phase, as the focus shifted from slowing transmission to ending the epidemic. On 8 April 2015, the WHO reported only 30 confirmed cases, the lowest weekly total since the third week of May 2014.

On 29 December 2015, 42 days after the last person tested negative for a second time, Guinea was declared free of Ebola transmission. At that time, a 90-day period of heightened surveillance was announced by that agency. "This is the first time that all three countries – Guinea, Liberia, and Sierra Leone – have stopped the original chains of transmission ...", the organization stated in a news release. A new case was detected in Sierra Leone on 14 January 2016. However, the outbreak was declared no longer an emergency on 29 March 2016.

2014 SPREAD OUTSIDE WEST AFRICA

On 19 September, Eric Duncan flew from his native Liberia to Texas; five days later he began showing symptoms and visited a hospital but was sent home. His condition worsened and he returned to the hospital on 28 September, where he died on 8 October. Health officials confirmed a diagnosis of Ebola on 30 September – the first case in the United States.

In early October, Teresa Romero, a 44-year-old Spanish nurse, contracted Ebola after caring for a priest who had been repatriated from West Africa. This was the first transmission of the virus to occur outside Africa. Romero tested negative for the disease on 20 October, suggesting that she may have recovered from an Ebola infection.

On 12 October, the Centers for Disease Control and Prevention (CDC) confirmed that a nurse in Texas, Nina Pham, who had treated Duncan tested positive for the Ebola virus, the first known case of transmission in the United States. On 15 October, a second Texas healthcare worker who had treated Duncan was confirmed to have the virus. Both of these people recovered. An unrelated case involved a doctor in New York City, who returned to the United States from Guinea after working with Médecins Sans Frontières and tested positive for Ebola on 23 October. The person recovered and was discharged from Bellevue Hospital on 11 November. On 24 December 2014, a laboratory in Atlanta, Georgia reported that a technician had been exposed to Ebola.

On 29 December 2014, Pauline Cafferkey, a British nurse who had just returned to Glasgow from Sierra Leone, was diagnosed with Ebola at Glasgow's Gartnavel General Hospital. After initial treatment in Glasgow, she was transferred by air to RAF Northolt, then to the specialist high-level isolation unit at the Royal Free Hospital in London for longer-term treatment.

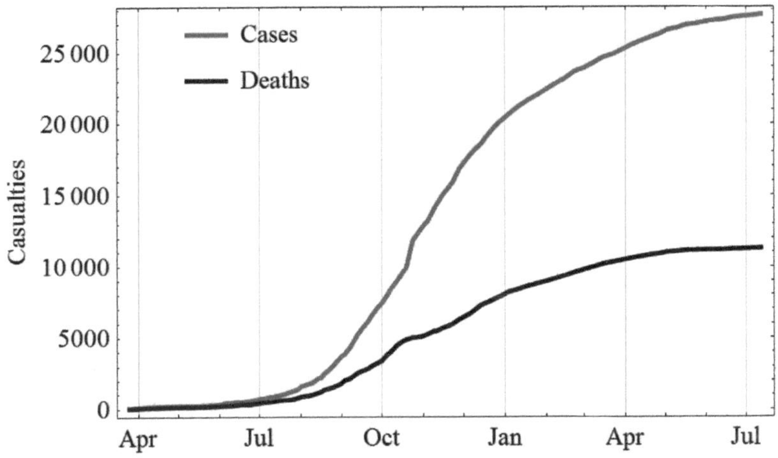

Fig. 8.2 Cases & Deaths during 2014 Outbreak

2018-2020 KIVU

On 1 August 2018, the world's 10th Ebola outbreak was declared in the North Kivu province of the Democratic Republic of the Congo. It was the first Ebola outbreak in a military conflict zone, with thousands of refugees in the area. By November 2018, nearly 200 Congolese had died of Ebola, about half of them from the city of Beni, where armed groups are fighting over the region's mineral wealth, impeding medical relief efforts.

By March 2019, this became the second-largest Ebola outbreak ever recorded, with more than 1,000 cases and insecurity continue to be the major resistance to providing an adequate response. As of 4 June 2019, the WHO reported 2025 confirmed and probable cases with 1357 deaths. In June 2019, two people died of Ebola in neighboring Uganda.

In July 2019, an infected man traveled to Goma, home to more than two million people. One week later, on 17 July 2019, the WHO declared the Ebola outbreak a global health emergency, the fifth time such a declaration has been made by the organization. A government spokesman said that half of the Ebola cases are unidentified, and he added that the current outbreak could last up to three years. On 25 June 2020, the second biggest EVD outbreak ever was declared over.

2021

GUINEA

In February 2021, Dr. Sakoba Keita, head of Guinea's national health agency confirmed that 3 people had died of Ebola in the south-eastern region near the city of Nzérékoré. A further 5 people also tested positive. Dr. Keita also confirmed more testing was underway and attempts to trace and isolate further cases had begun. On 14 February, the Guinean government declared an Ebola epidemic. The outbreak may have started following the reactivation of a latent case in a survivor of an earlier outbreak. As of 4 May 2021, 23 cases were reported, with no new cases or deaths since 3 April 2021. A 42-day countdown period was started on 8 May 2021, and on 19 June, the outbreak was declared over.

IVORY COAST

On 14 August 2021, The Ministry of Health of Cote d'Ivoire confirmed the country's first case of Ebola since 1994. This came after the Institut Pasteur in Cote d'Ivoire confirmed the Ebola Virus Disease in samples collected from a patient, who was hospitalized in the commercial capital of Abidjan, after arriving from Guinea. However, on 31 August 2021, the WHO found that, after further tests in a laboratory in Lyon, the patient did not have Ebola. The cause of her disease is still being analyzed.

KEY FACTS

- Ebola virus disease (EVD), formerly known as Ebola hemorrhagic fever, is a rare but severe, often fatal illness in humans.
- The virus is transmitted to people from wild animals and spreads in the human population through human-to-human transmission.
- The average EVD case fatality rate is around 50%. Case fatality rates have varied from 25% to 90% in past outbreaks.
- Community engagement is key to successfully controlling outbreaks.
- Good outbreak control relies on applying a package of interventions, namely case management, infection prevention and control practices, surveillance and contact tracing, a good laboratory service, safe and dignified burials, and social mobilization.
- Vaccines to protect against Ebola have been developed and have been used to help control the spread of Ebola outbreaks in Guinea and in the Democratic Republic of the Congo (DRC).
- Early supportive care with rehydration, symptomatic treatment improves survival. Two monoclonal antibodies (Inmazeb and Ebanga) were approved for the treatment of Zaire ebolavirus (Ebolavirus) infection in adults and children by the US Food and Drug Administration in late 2020.

CHAPTER NINE

THE CORONAVIRUS PANDEMIC

Coronaviruses are a group of related RNA viruses that cause diseases in mammals and birds. In humans and birds, they cause respiratory tract infections that can range from mild to lethal. Mild illnesses in humans include some cases of the common cold (which is also caused by other viruses, predominantly rhinoviruses), while more lethal varieties can cause SARS, MERS, and COVID-19, which is causing an ongoing pandemic. In cows and pigs, they cause diarrhea, while in mice they cause hepatitis and encephalomyelitis.

Coronaviruses constitute the subfamily Orthocoronavirinae, in the family Coronaviridae, order Nidovirales and realm Riboviria. They have enveloped viruses with a positive-sense single-stranded RNA genome and a nucleocapsid of helical symmetry. The genome size of coronaviruses ranges from approximately 26 to 32 kilobases, one of the largest among RNA viruses. They have characteristic club-shaped spikes that project from their surface, which in electron micrographs create an image reminiscent of the solar corona, from which their name derives.

ETYMOLOGY

The name "coronavirus" is derived from Latin corona, meaning "crown" or "wreath", itself a borrowing from Greek κορώνη korṓnē, "garland, wreath". The name was coined by June Almeida and David Tyrrell who first observed and studied human coronaviruses. The word was first used in print in 1968 by an informal group of virologists in the journal Nature to designate the new family of viruses. The name refers to the characteristic appearance of virions (the infective form of the virus) by electron microscopy, which has a fringe of large, bulbous surface projections creating an image reminiscent of the solar corona or halo. This morphology is created by the viral spike peplomers, which are proteins on the surface of the virus.

The scientific name Coronavirus was accepted as a genus name by the International Committee for the Nomenclature of Viruses (later renamed International Committee on Taxonomy of Viruses) in 1971. As the number of new species increased, the genus was split into four genera, namely Alphacoronavirus, Betacoronavirus, Deltacoronavirus, and Gammacoronavirus in 2009. The common name coronavirus is used to refer to any member of the subfamily Orthocoronavirinae. As of 2020, 45 species are officially recognized.

HISTORY

The earliest reports of coronavirus infection in animals occurred in the late 1920s when an acute respiratory infection of domesticated chickens emerged in North America. Arthur Schalk and M.C. Hawn in 1931 made the first detailed report which described a new respiratory infection of chickens in North Dakota. The infection of newborn chicks was characterized by gasping and listlessness with high mortality rates of 40–90%. Leland David Bushnell and Carl Alfred Brandly isolated the virus that caused the infection in 1933. The virus was then known as infectious bronchitis virus (IBV). Charles D. Hudson and Fred Robert Beaudette cultivated the virus for the first time in 1937. The specimen came to be known as the Beaudette strain. In the late 1940s, two more animal coronaviruses, JHM which causes brain disease (murine encephalitis), and mouse hepatitis virus (MHV) that causes hepatitis in mice were discovered. It was not realized at the time that these three different viruses were related.

Human coronaviruses were discovered in the 1960s using two different methods in the United Kingdom and the United States. E.C. Kendall, Malcolm Bynoe, and David Tyrrell working at the Common Cold Unit of the British Medical Research Council collected a unique common cold virus designated B814 in 1961. The virus could not be cultivated using standard techniques which had successfully cultivated rhinoviruses, adenoviruses, and other known common cold viruses. In 1965, Tyrrell and Bynoe successfully cultivated the novel virus by serially passing it through the organ culture of the human embryonic trachea. The new cultivating method was introduced to the lab by Bertil Hoorn. The isolated virus when intranasally inoculated into volunteers caused a cold and was inactivated by ether which indicated it had a lipid envelope. Dorothy Hamre and John Procknow at the University of Chicago isolated a novel cold from medical students in 1962. They isolated and grew the virus in kidney tissue culture, designating it 229E. The novel virus caused a cold in volunteers and, like B814, was inactivated by ether.

Virologist June Almeida at St Thomas Hospital in London, collaborating with Tyrrell, compared the structures of IBV, B814, and 229E in 1967. Using electron microscopy the three viruses were shown to be morphologically related by their general shape and distinctive club-like spikes. A research group at the National Institute of Health the same year was able to isolate another member of this new group of viruses using organ culture and named one of the samples OC43 (OC for organ culture). Like B814, 229E, and IBV, the novel cold virus OC43 had distinctive club-like spikes when observed with the electron microscope.

The IBV-like novel cold viruses were soon shown to be also morphologically related to the mouse hepatitis virus. This new group of viruses was named coronaviruses after their distinctive morphological appearance. Human coronavirus 229E and human coronavirus OC43 continued to be studied in subsequent decades. The coronavirus strain B814 was lost. It is not known which present human coronavirus it was. Other human coronaviruses have since been identified, including SARS-CoV in 2003, HCoV NL63 in 2003, HCoV HKU1 in 2004, MERS-CoV in 2013, and SARS-CoV-2 in 2019. There have also been a large number of animal coronaviruses identified since the 1960s.

MICROBIOLOGY

STRUCTURE

Coronaviruses are large, roughly spherical particles with unique surface projections. Their size is highly variable with average diameters of 80 to 120 nm. Extreme sizes are known from 50 to 200 nm in diameter. The total molecular mass is on average 40,000 kDa. They are enclosed in an envelope embedded with a number of protein molecules. The lipid bilayer envelope, membrane proteins, and nucleocapsid protect the virus when it is outside the host cell.

The viral envelope is made up of a lipid bilayer in which the membrane (M), envelope (E), and spike (S) structural proteins are anchored. The molar ratio of E:S:M in the lipid bilayer is approximately 1:20:300. The E and M proteins are the structural proteins that combined with the lipid bilayer to shape the viral envelope and maintain its size. S proteins are needed for interaction with the host cells. But human coronavirus NL63 is peculiar in that its M protein has the binding site for the host cell and not its S protein. The diameter of the envelope is 85 nm. The envelope of the virus in electron micrographs appears as a distinct pair of electron-dense shells (shells that are relatively opaque to the electron beam used to scan the virus particle).

The M protein is the main structural protein of the envelope that provides the overall shape and is a type III membrane protein. It consists of 218 to 263 amino acid residues and forms a layer 7.8 nm thick. It has three domains, a short N-terminal ectodomain, a triple-spanning transmembrane domain, and a C-terminal endodomain. The C-terminal domain forms a matrix-like lattice that adds to the extra-thickness of the envelope. Different species can have either N- or O-linked glycans in their protein amino-terminal domain. The M protein is crucial during the assembly, budding, envelope formation, and pathogenesis stages of the virus lifecycle.

The E proteins are minor structural proteins and highly variable in different species. There are only about 20 copies of the E protein molecule in a coronavirus particle. They are 8.4 to 12 kDa in size and are composed of 76 to 109 amino acids. They are integral proteins (i.e. embedded in the lipid layer) and have two domains namely a transmembrane domain and an extramembrane C-terminal domain. They are almost fully α-helical, with a single α-helical transmembrane domain, and form pentameric (five-molecular) ion channels in the lipid bilayer. They are responsible for virion assembly, intracellular trafficking, and morphogenesis (budding).

The spikes are the most distinguishing feature of coronaviruses and are responsible for the corona- or halo-like surface. On average a coronavirus particle has 74 surface spikes. Each spike is about 20 nm long and is composed of a trimer of the S protein. The S protein is in turn composed of an S1 and S2 subunit. The homotrimeric S protein is a class I fusion protein that mediates the receptor binding and membrane fusion between the virus and host cell. The S1 subunit forms the head of the spike and has the receptor-binding domain (RBD). The S2 subunit forms the stem which anchors the spike in the viral envelope and protease activation enables fusion. The two subunits remain noncovalently linked as they are exposed to the viral surface until they attach to the host cell membrane. In a functionally active state, three S1 are attached to two S2 subunits. The subunit complex is split into individual subunits when the virus binds and fuses with the host cell under the action of proteases such as the cathepsin family and transmembrane protease serine 2 (TMPRSS2) of the host cell.

S1 proteins are the most critical components in terms of infection. They are also the most variable components as they are responsible for host cell specificity. They possess two major domains named N-terminal domain (S1-NTD) and C-terminal domain (S1-CTD), both of which serve as the receptor-binding domains. The NTDs recognize and bind sugars on the surface of the host cell. An exception is the MHV NTD that binds to a protein receptor carcinoembryonic antigen-related cell adhesion molecule 1 (CEACAM1). S1-CTDs are responsible for recognizing different protein receptors such as angiotensin-converting enzyme 2 (ACE2), aminopeptidase N (APN), and dipeptidyl peptidase 4 (DPP4).

A subset of coronaviruses (specifically the members of betacoronavirus subgroup A) also has a shorter spike-like surface protein called hemagglutinin esterase (HE). The HE proteins occur as homodimers composed of about 400 amino acid residues and are 40 to 50 kDa in size. They appear as tiny surface projections of 5 to 7 nm long embedded in between the spikes. They help in the attachment to and detachment from the host cell.

Inside the envelope, there is the nucleocapsid, which is formed from multiple copies of the nucleocapsid (N) protein, which are bound to the positive-sense single-stranded RNA genome in a continuous beads-on-a-string type conformation. N protein is a phosphoprotein of 43 to 50 kDa in size and is divided into three conserved domains. The majority of the protein is made up of domains 1 and 2, which are typically rich in arginines and lysines. Domain 3 has a short carboxy-terminal end and has a net negative charge due to excess acidic over basic amino acid residues.

GENOME

Coronaviruses contain a positive-sense, single-stranded RNA genome. The genome size for coronaviruses ranges from 26.4 to 31.7 kilobases. The genome size is one of the largest among RNA viruses. The genome has a 5′ methylated cap and a 3′

polyadenylated tail.

The genome organization for a coronavirus is 5′-leader-UTR-replicase (ORF1ab)-spike (S)-envelope (E)-membrane (M)-nucleocapsid (N)-3′UTR-poly (A) tail. The open reading frames 1a and 1b, which occupy the first two-thirds of the genome, encode the replicase polyprotein (pp1ab). The replicase polyprotein self cleaves to form 16 nonstructural proteins (nsp1–nsp16).

The later reading frames encode the four major structural proteins: spike, envelope, membrane, and nucleocapsid. Interspersed between these reading frames are the reading frames for the accessory proteins. The number of accessory proteins and their function is unique depending on the specific coronavirus.

REPLICATION CYCLE

CELL ENTRY

Infection begins when the viral spike protein attaches to its complementary host cell receptor. After attachment, a protease of the host cell cleaves and activates the receptor-attached spike protein. Depending on the host cell protease available, cleavage and activation allow the virus to enter the host cell by endocytosis or direct fusion of the viral envelope with the host membrane.

GENOME TRANSLATION

On entry into the host cell, the virus particle is uncoated, and its genome enters the cell cytoplasm. The coronavirus RNA genome has a 5′ methylated cap and a 3′ polyadenylated tail, which allows it to act as a messenger RNA and be directly translated by the host cell's ribosomes. The host ribosomes translate the initial overlapping open reading frames ORF1a and ORF1b of the virus genome into two large overlapping polyproteins, pp1a and pp1ab.

The larger polyprotein pp1ab is a result of a -1 ribosomal frameshift caused by a slippery sequence (UUUAAAC) and a downstream RNA pseudoknot at the end of open reading frame ORF1a. The ribosomal frameshift allows for the continuous translation of ORF1a followed by ORF1b.

The polyproteins have their own proteases, PLpro (nsp3) and 3CLpro (nsp5), which cleave the polyproteins at different specific sites. The cleavage of polyprotein pp1ab yields 16 nonstructural proteins (nsp1 to nsp16). Product proteins include various replication proteins such as RNA-dependent RNA polymerase (nsp12), RNA helicase (nsp13), and exoribonuclease (nsp14).

REPLICASE-TRANSCRIPTASE

A number of the nonstructural proteins coalesce to form a multi-protein replicase-transcriptase complex (RTC). The main replicase-transcriptase protein is the RNA-dependent RNA polymerase (RdRp). It is directly involved in the replication and transcription of RNA from an RNA strand. The other nonstructural proteins in the complex assist in the replication and transcription process. The exoribonuclease nonstructural protein, for instance, provides extra fidelity to replication by providing a proofreading function that the RNA-dependent RNA polymerase lacks.

Replication – One of the main functions of the complex is to replicate the viral genome. RdRp directly mediates the synthesis of negative-sense genomic RNA from the positive-sense genomic RNA. This is followed by the replication of positive-sense genomic RNA from the negative-sense genomic RNA.

Transcription – The other important function of the complex is to transcribe the viral genome. RdRp directly mediates the synthesis of negative-sense subgenomic RNA molecules from the positive-sense genomic RNA. This process is followed by the transcription of these negative-sense subgenomic RNA molecules to their corresponding positive-sense mRNAs. The subgenomic mRNAs form a "nested set" which has a common 5‘-head and partially duplicate 3'-end.

Recombination – The replicase-transcriptase complex is also capable of genetic recombination when at least two viral genomes are present in the same infected cell. RNA recombination appears to be a major driving force in determining genetic variability within a coronavirus species, the capability of a coronavirus species to jump from one host to another, and, infrequently, in determining the emergence of novel coronaviruses. The exact mechanism of recombination in coronaviruses is unclear but likely involves template switching during genome replication.

ASSEMBLY AND RELEASE

The replicated positive-sense genomic RNA becomes the genome of the progeny viruses. The mRNAs are gene transcripts of the last third of the virus genome after the initial overlapping reading frame. These mRNAs are translated by the host's ribosomes into the structural proteins and many accessory proteins. RNA translation occurs inside the endoplasmic reticulum. The viral structural proteins S, E, and M move along the secretory pathway into the Golgi intermediate compartment. There, the M proteins direct most protein-protein interactions required for the assembly of viruses following its binding to the nucleocapsid. Progeny viruses are then released from the host cell by exocytosis through secretory vesicles. Once released the viruses can infect other host cells.

TRANSMISSION

Infected carriers are able to shed viruses into the environment. The interaction of the coronavirus spike protein with its complementary cell receptor is central in determining the tissue tropism, infectivity, and species range of the released virus. Coronaviruses mainly target epithelial cells. They are transmitted from one host to another host, depending on the coronavirus species, by either an aerosol, fomite or fecal-oral route.

Human coronaviruses infect the epithelial cells of the respiratory tract, while animal coronaviruses generally infect the epithelial cells of the digestive tract. SARS coronavirus, for example, infects the human epithelial cells of the lungs via an aerosol route by binding to the angiotensin-converting enzyme 2 (ACE2) receptor. Transmissible gastroenteritis coronavirus (TGEV) infects the pig epithelial cells of the digestive tract via a fecal-oral route by binding to the alanine aminopeptidase (APN) receptor.

ORIGIN

The most recent common ancestor (MRCA) of all coronaviruses is estimated to have existed as recently as 8000 BCE, although some models place the common ancestor as far back as 55 million years or more, implying long term coevolution with bat and avian species. The most recent common ancestor of the alphacoronavirus line has been placed at about 2400 BCE, of the betacoronavirus line at 3300 BCE, of the gammacoronavirus line at 2800 BCE, and the delta coronavirus line at about 3000 BCE. Bats and birds, as warm-blooded flying vertebrates, are an ideal natural reservoir for the coronavirus gene pool (with bats the reservoir for alpha coronaviruses and betacoronavirus – and birds the reservoir for gammacoronaviruses and delta coronaviruses). The large number and global range of bat and avian species that host viruses have enabled extensive evolution and dissemination of coronaviruses.

Many human coronaviruses have their origin in bats. The human coronavirus NL63 shared a common ancestor with a bat coronavirus (ARCoV.2) between 1190 and 1449 CE. The human coronavirus 229E shared a common ancestor with a bat coronavirus (GhanaGrp1 Bt CoV) between 1686 and 1800 CE. More recently, alpaca coronavirus and human coronavirus 229E diverged sometime before 1960. MERS-CoV emerged in humans from bats through the intermediate host of camels. MERS-CoV, although related to several bat coronavirus species, appears to have diverged from these several centuries ago. The most closely related bat coronavirus and SARS-CoV diverged in 1986. The ancestors of SARS-CoV first infected leaf-nose bats of the genus Hipposideridae; subsequently, they spread to horseshoe bats in the species Rhinolophidae, then to Asian palm civets, and finally to humans.

Unlike other beta coronaviruses, bovine coronavirus of the species Betacoronavirus 1 and subgenus Embecovirus is thought to have originated in rodents and not in bats. In the 1790s, equine coronavirus diverged from the bovine coronavirus after a cross-species jump. Later in the 1890s, human coronavirus OC43 diverged from bovine coronavirus after another cross-species spillover event. It is speculated that the flu pandemic of 1890 may have been caused by this spillover event, and not by the influenza virus, because of the related timing, neurological symptoms, and unknown causative agent of the pandemic. Besides causing respiratory infections, human coronavirus OC43 is also suspected of playing a role in neurological diseases. In the 1950s, the human coronavirus OC43 began to diverge into its present genotypes. Phylogenetically, mouse hepatitis virus (Murine coronavirus), which infects the mouse's liver and central nervous system, is related to human coronavirus OC43 and bovine coronavirus. Human coronavirus HKU1, like the aforementioned viruses, also has its origins in rodents.

INFECTION IN HUMANS

Coronaviruses vary significantly in risk factor. Some can kill more than 30% of those infected, such as MERS-CoV, and some are relatively harmless, such as the common cold. Coronaviruses can cause colds with major symptoms, such as fever, and a sore throat from swollen adenoids. Coronaviruses can cause pneumonia (either direct viral pneumonia or secondary bacterial pneumonia) and bronchitis (either direct viral bronchitis or secondary bacterial bronchitis). The human coronavirus discovered in 2003, SARS-CoV, which causes severe acute respiratory syndrome (SARS), has a unique pathogenesis because it causes both upper and lower respiratory tract infections.

Six species of human coronaviruses are known, with one species subdivided into two different strains, making seven strains of human coronaviruses altogether. Seasonal distribution of HCoV-NL63 in Germany shows a preferential detection from November to March.

Four human coronaviruses produce symptoms that are generally mild, even though it is contended they might have been more aggressive in the past:

Human coronavirus OC43 (HCoV-OC43), β-CoV

Human coronavirus HKU1 (HCoV-HKU1), β-CoV

Human coronavirus 229E (HCoV-229E), α-CoV

Human coronavirus NL63 (HCoV-NL63), α-CoV

Three human coronaviruses produce potentially severe symptoms:

Severe acute respiratory syndrome coronavirus (SARS-CoV), β-CoV (identified in 2003)

The Middle East respiratory syndrome-related coronavirus (MERS-CoV), β-CoV (identified in 2012)

Severe acute respiratory syndrome coronavirus 2 (SARS-CoV-2), β-CoV (identified in 2019)

These cause the diseases commonly called SARS, MERS, and COVID-19 respectively.

COMMON COLD

Although the common cold is usually caused by rhinoviruses, in about 15% of cases the cause is a coronavirus. The human coronaviruses HCoV-OC43, HCoV-HKU1, HCoV-229E, and HCoV-NL63 continually circulate in the human population in adults and children worldwide and produce the generally mild symptoms of the common cold. The four mild coronaviruses have a seasonal incidence occurring in the winter months in temperate climates. There is no preponderance in any season in tropical climates.

SEVERE ACUTE RESPIRATORY SYNDROME (SARS)

Severe acute respiratory syndrome (SARS) is a viral respiratory disease of zoonotic origin caused by severe acute respiratory syndrome coronavirus (SARS-CoV or SARS-CoV-1), the first identified strain of the SARS coronavirus species severe acute respiratory syndrome-related coronavirus (SARSr-CoV). The first known cases occurred in November 2002, and the syndrome caused the 2002–2004 SARS outbreak. Around late 2017, Chinese scientists traced the virus through the intermediary of Asian palm civets to cave-dwelling horseshoe bats in Xiyang Yi Ethnic Township, Yunnan.

SARS was a relatively rare disease; at the end of the epidemic in June 2003, the incidence was 8,469 cases with a case fatality rate (CFR) of 11%. No cases of SARS-CoV-1 have been reported worldwide since 2004.

In December 2019, another strain of SARS-CoV was identified as severe acute respiratory syndrome coronavirus 2 (SARS-CoV-2). This new strain causes coronavirus disease 2019 (COVID-19), a disease that brought about the COVID-19 pandemic.

In 2003, following the outbreak of severe acute respiratory syndrome (SARS) which had begun the prior year in Asia, and secondary cases elsewhere in the world, the World Health Organization (WHO) issued a press release stating that a novel coronavirus identified by several laboratories was the causative agent for SARS. The virus was officially named the SARS coronavirus (SARS-CoV). More than 8,000 people from 29 different countries and territories were infected, and at least 774 died.

MIDDLE EAST RESPIRATORY SYNDROME (MERS)

In September 2012, a new type of coronavirus was identified, initially called Novel Coronavirus 2012, and now officially named Middle East respiratory syndrome coronavirus (MERS-CoV). The World Health Organization issued a global alert soon after. The WHO update on 28 September 2012 said the virus did not seem to pass easily from person to person. However, on 12 May 2013, a case of human-to-human transmission in France was confirmed by the French Ministry of Social Affairs and Health. In addition, cases of human-to-human transmission were reported by the Ministry of Health in Tunisia. Two confirmed cases involved people who seemed to have caught the disease from their late father, who became ill after a visit to Qatar and Saudi Arabia. Despite this, it appears the virus had trouble spreading from human to human, as most individuals who are infected do not transmit the virus. By 30 October 2013, there were 124 cases and 52 deaths in Saudi Arabia.

After the Dutch Erasmus Medical Centre sequenced the virus, the virus was given a new name, Human Coronavirus–Erasmus Medical Centre (HCoV-EMC). The final name for the virus is Middle East respiratory syndrome coronavirus (MERS-CoV). The only U.S. cases (both survived) were recorded in May 2014.

In May 2015, an outbreak of MERS-CoV occurred in the Republic of Korea, when a man who had traveled to the Middle East, visited four hospitals in the Seoul area to treat his illness. This caused one of the largest outbreaks of MERS-CoV outside the Middle East. As of December 2019, 2,468 cases of MERS-CoV infection had been confirmed by laboratory tests, 851 of which were fatal, a mortality rate of approximately 34.5%.

COVID-19

Coronavirus disease 2019 (COVID-19) is a contagious disease caused by severe acute respiratory syndrome coronavirus 2 (SARS-CoV-2). The first known case was identified in Wuhan, China, in December 2019. The disease has since spread worldwide, leading to an ongoing pandemic.

Symptoms of COVID-19 are variable, but often include fever, cough, headache, fatigue, breathing difficulties, and loss of smell and taste. Symptoms may begin one to fourteen days after exposure to the virus. At least a third of people who are infected do not develop noticeable symptoms. Of those people who develop symptoms noticeable enough to be classed as patients, most (81%) develop mild to moderate symptoms (up to mild pneumonia), while 14% develop severe symptoms (dyspnea, hypoxia, or more than 50% lung involvement on imaging), and 5% suffer critical symptoms (respiratory failure, shock, or multiorgan dysfunction). Older people are at a higher risk of developing severe symptoms. Some people continue to experience a range of effects (long COVID) for months after recovery, and damage to organs has been observed. Multi-year studies are underway to further investigate the long-term effects of the disease.

COVID-19 transmits when people breathe in air contaminated by droplets and small airborne particles containing the virus. The risk of breathing these in is highest when people are in close proximity, but they can be inhaled over longer distances, particularly indoors. Transmission can also occur if splashed or sprayed with contaminated fluids in the eyes, nose, or mouth, and, rarely, via contaminated surfaces. People remain contagious for up to 20 days and can spread the virus even if they do not develop symptoms.

Several testing methods have been developed to diagnose the disease. The standard diagnostic method is by detection of the virus's nucleic acid by real-time reverse transcription-polymerase chain reaction (rRT-PCR), transcription-mediated amplification (TMA), or by reverse transcription loop-mediated isothermal amplification (RT-LAMP) from a nasopharyngeal swab.

Several COVID-19 vaccines have been approved and distributed in various countries, which have initiated mass vaccination campaigns. Other preventive measures include physical or social distancing, quarantining, ventilation of indoor spaces, covering coughs and sneezes, hand washing, and keeping unwashed hands away from the face. The use of face masks or coverings has been recommended in public settings to minimize the risk of transmissions. While work is underway to develop drugs that inhibit the virus, the primary treatment is symptomatic. Management involves the treatment of symptoms, supportive care, isolation, and experimental measures.

9 798885 696722

Printed by Libri Plureos GmbH in Hamburg, Germany